Heterogeneous Computing

ACM Books

Editor in Chief

M. Tamer Özsu, *University of Waterloo*

ACM Books is a series of high-quality books for the computer science community, published by ACM and many in collaboration with Morgan & Claypool Publishers. ACM Books publications are widely distributed in both print and digital formats through booksellers and to libraries (and library consortia) and individual ACM members via the ACM Digital Library platform.

Heterogeneous Computing: Hardware and Software Perspectives

Mohamed Zahran, *New York University*
2019

Making Databases Work: The Pragmatic Wisdom of Michael Stonebraker

Editor: Michael L. Brodie
2018

The Handbook of Multimodal-Multisensor Interfaces, Volume 2: Signal Processing, Architectures, and Detection of Emotion and Cognition

Editors: Sharon Oviatt, *Monash University*
Björn Schuller, *University of Augsburg and Imperial College London*
Philip R. Cohen, *Monash University*
Daniel Sonntag, *German Research Center for Artificial Intelligence (DFKI)*
Gerasimos Potamianos, *University of Thessaly*
Antonio Krüger, *Saarland University and German Research Center for Artificial Intelligence (DFKI)*
2018

Declarative Logic Programming: Theory, Systems, and Applications

Editors: Michael Kifer, *Stony Brook University*
Yanhong Annie Liu, *Stony Brook University*
2018

The Sparse Fourier Transform: Theory and Practice

Haitham Hassanieh, *University of Illinois at Urbana-Champaign*
2018

The Continuing Arms Race: Code-Reuse Attacks and Defenses

Editors: Per Larsen, *Immunant, Inc.*
Ahmad-Reza Sadeghi, *Technische Universität Darmstadt*
2018

Frontiers of Multimedia Research
Editor: Shih-Fu Chang, *Columbia University*
2018

Shared-Memory Parallelism Can Be Simple, Fast, and Scalable
Julian Shun, *University of California, Berkeley*
2017

Computational Prediction of Protein Complexes from Protein Interaction
Networks
Sriganesh Srihari, *The University of Queensland Institute for Molecular Bioscience*
Chern Han Yong, *Duke-National University of Singapore Medical School*
Limsoon Wong, *National University of Singapore*
2017

The Handbook of Multimodal-Multisensor Interfaces, Volume 1:
Foundations, User Modeling, and Common Modality Combinations
Editors: Sharon Oviatt, *Incaa Designs*
Björn Schuller, *University of Passau and Imperial College London*
Philip R. Cohen, *Voicebox Technologies*
Daniel Sonntag, *German Research Center for Artificial Intelligence (DFKI)*
Gerasimos Potamianos, *University of Thessaly*
Antonio Krüger, *Saarland University and German Research Center for Artificial Intelligence
(DFKI)*
2017

Communities of Computing: Computer Science and Society in the ACM
Thomas J. Misa, Editor, *University of Minnesota*
2017

Text Data Management and Analysis: A Practical Introduction to Information
Retrieval and Text Mining
ChengXiang Zhai, *University of Illinois at Urbana–Champaign*
Sean Massung, *University of Illinois at Urbana–Champaign*
2016

An Architecture for Fast and General Data Processing on Large Clusters
Matei Zaharia, *Stanford University*
2016

Reactive Internet Programming: State Chart XML in Action
Franck Barbier, *University of Pau, France*
2016

Verified Functional Programming in Agda
Aaron Stump, *The University of Iowa*
2016

The VR Book: Human-Centered Design for Virtual Reality
Jason Jerald, *NextGen Interactions*
2016

Ada's Legacy: Cultures of Computing from the Victorian to the Digital Age
Robin Hammerman, *Stevens Institute of Technology*
Andrew L. Russell, *Stevens Institute of Technology*
2016

Edmund Berkeley and the Social Responsibility of Computer Professionals
Bernadette Longo, *New Jersey Institute of Technology*
2015

Candidate Multilinear Maps
Sanjam Garg, *University of California, Berkeley*
2015

Smarter Than Their Machines: Oral Histories of Pioneers in Interactive Computing
John Cullinane, *Northeastern University; Mossavar-Rahmani Center for Business and Government, John F. Kennedy School of Government, Harvard University*
2015

A Framework for Scientific Discovery through Video Games
Seth Cooper, *University of Washington*
2014

Trust Extension as a Mechanism for Secure Code Execution on Commodity Computers
Bryan Jeffrey Parno, *Microsoft Research*
2014

Embracing Interference in Wireless Systems
Shyamnath Gollakota, *University of Washington*
2014

Heterogeneous Computing

Hardware and Software Perspectives

Mohamed Zahran

New York University

ACM Books #26

Heterogeneous Computing: Hardware and Software Perspectives
Mohamed Zahran

books.acm.org
http://books.acm.org

ISBN: 978-1-4503-6097-5   hardcover
ISBN: 978-1-4503-6233-7   paperback
ISBN: 978-1-4503-6100-2   eBook
ISBN: 978-1-4503-6098-2   ePub

Series ISSN: 2374-6769 print   2374-6777 electronic

DOIs:

10.1145/3281649 Book
10.1145/3281649.3281650 Preface
10.1145/3281649.3281651 Chapter 1
10.1145/3281649.3281652 Chapter 2

10.1145/3281649.3281653 Chapter 3
10.1145/3281649.3281654 Chapter 4
10.1145/3281649.3281655 Chapter 5
10.1145/3281649.3281656 References/Index/Bio

A publication in the ACM Books series, #26
Editor in Chief: M. Tamer Özsu, *University of Waterloo*

This book was typeset in Arnhem Pro 10/14 and Flama using ZzTEX.
First Edition
10 9 8 7 6 5 4 3 2 1

To my family, without whom I wouldn't have existed in the first place and wouldn't have managed through this life.

Contents

Preface   xiii

Chapter 1   Why Are We Forced to Deal with Heterogeneous Computing?   1

1.1   The Power Issue   2
1.2   Heterogeneity beyond Our Control   5
1.3   Heterogeneity within Our Control   9
1.4   Seems Like Part of a Solution to Exascale Computing   11

Chapter 2   Different Players: Heterogeneity in Computing   13

2.1   Multicore   14
2.2   GPUs   17
2.3   FPGA   23
2.4   Automata Processors   24
2.5   Neuromorphic Chips   25
2.6   Other Accelerators   26
2.7   Mix-and-Match   28
2.8   In Conclusion   32

Chapter 3   Architecture: Heterogeneity in Design   33

3.1   Memory System   33
3.2   Interconnect   35
3.3   Examples of Supercomputers   43
3.4   Security Challenges Facing Heterogeneous Computing   46
3.5   Bandwidth   50
3.6   In Conclusion   65

Chapter 4   **Programmability**   67

    4.1   Wish List of a Programmer   67

    4.2   Psychology of Programming   69

    4.3   What Do We Have? The Current Status Quo   71

    4.4   In Conclusion   88

Chapter 5   **Research Directions**   91

    5.1   Processing-in-Memory (PIM) / Near-Data Processing (NDP)   91

    5.2   Exascale Computing   92

    5.3   Neuromorphic Chips   92

    5.4   Quantum Computing   95

References   97

Index   111

Author's Biography   113

Preface

The term *heterogeneous computing* has become famous lately (lately, meaning in the last five years!). It started infiltrating many articles. Research papers have been, and are still being, written about heterogeneous computing and its implications on both software and hardware. The definition of this term is quite straightforward: *executing programs on a computing platform with computing nodes of different characteristics.* What is tricky is whether this is a good thing or a bad thing.

From a hardware perspective, as we will see later in this book, it is a good thing. Each computing node is efficient in specific types of applications. Efficiency here means it gets the best performance (e.g., speed) with lowest cost (e.g., power). This excellence in price-performance is very much needed in our current era of big data, severe power consumption, and the road to exascale computing. So if we can assign to each node the part of the program that it excels at, then we get the results of price-performance, and this is the main challenge facing the software community.

From a software perspective, heterogeneous computing seems like bad news because it makes programming much more challenging. As a developer, you have way more tasks than with traditional homogeneous computing. You need to know about different execution units, or at least learn about the computing nodes in the system you are writing code for. Then you need to pick algorithms to make your program, or different parts of your program, suitable for these nodes. Finally, you need to tweak your code to get the needed performance by overcoming many bottlenecks that certainly exist in heterogeneous computing, like communication overhead between the different units, overhead of creating threads or processes, management of memory access of those different units, and so on.

We cannot then say that heterogeneous computing is good or bad news. But we can say that heterogeneous computing is now the norm and not the exception. It is here, it will continue to be here, and we need to deal with it. But how do we deal with it? This is the topic of this book.

This book discusses the topic of heterogeneous computing from different angles: hardware challenges, current hardware state-of-the-art, software issues, how to make the best use of the current heterogeneous systems, and what lies ahead. All the systems we use, from portable devices to supercomputers, embody some type of heterogeneity. The main reason for that is to have good performance with power efficiency. However, this opens the door to many challenges that we need to deal with at all levels of the computing stack: from algorithms all the way to process technology. The aim of this book is to introduce heterogeneous computing in the big picture. Whether you are a hardware designer or a software developer, you need to know how the pieces of the puzzle fit together.

This book will discuss several architecture designs of heterogeneous systems, the role of operating systems, and the need for more efficient programming models. The main goal is to bring researchers and engineers to the forefront of the research frontier in the new era that started a few years ago and is expected to continue for decades.

Acknowledgments

First and foremost, I would like to thank all my family for their support, encouragement, and unconditional love. I would like to thank Steve Welch, who is actually the one who gave me the idea of writing this book. A big thank you goes also to Tamer Özsu, the Editor in Chief of ACM Books, for his encouragement, flexibility, and willingness to answer many questions. Without him, this book wouldn't have seen the light of day.

Anything I have learned in my scientific endeavors is due to my professors, my students, and my colleagues. I cannot thank them enough. Dear students, we learn from you as much as you learn from us.

I would like also to thank Paul C. Anagnostopoulos and the entire copyediting team, who got the book into much better shape than my initial version. A thank you is also due to Achi Dosanjh, Barbara Ryan, and Bernadette Shade from ACM for their great help in the last stages of this book.

Mohamed Zahran
December 2018

1

Why Are We Forced to Deal with Heterogeneous Computing?

When computers were first built, about seven decades ago, there was one item on the wish list: correctness. Then soon a second wish appeared: speed. The notion of speed differs of course from those old days and applications to today's requirements. But in general we can say that we want fast execution. After a few more decades and the proliferation of desktop PCs and then laptops, power became the third wish, whether in the context of battery life or electricity bills. As computers infiltrated many fields and were used in many applications, like military and health care, we were forced to add a fourth wish: reliability. We do not want a computer to fail during a medical procedure, for example; or it would have been a big loss (financially and scientifically) if the rover Curiosity, which NASA landed on Mars in 2012, failed. (And yes, Curiosity is a computer.) With the interconnected world we are in today, security became a must. And this is the fifth wish. Correctness, speed, power, reliability, and security are the five main wishes we want from any computer system. The order of the items differs based on the application, societal needs, and the market segment. This wish list is what directs the advances in hardware and software. But the enabling technologies for fulfilling this wish list lie in hardware advances and software evolution. So there is a vicious cycle between the wish list and hardware and software advances, and this cycle is affected by societal needs. This chapter explains the changes we have been through from the dawn of computer systems till today that made heterogeneous computing a must.

In this chapter we see how computing systems evolved till the current status quo. We learn about the concept of heterogeneity and how to make use of it. At the end of this chapter, ask yourself: Have we reached heterogeneous computing willingly? Or against our will? I hope by then you will have an answer.

1.1 The Power Issue

In 1965 Gordon Moore, cofounder of Intel together with Robert Noyce, published a four-page paper that became very famous [Moore 1965]. This paper, titled "Cramming More Components onto Integrated Circuits," made a prediction that the number of components (he did not mention transistors specifically, but the prediction evolved to mean transistors) in an integrated circuit (IC) will double every year. This prediction evolved over time to be two years, then settled on 18 months. This is what we call *Moore's law*: transistors on a chip are expected to double every 18 months. The 50th anniversary of Moore's law was in 2015! More transistors per chip means more features, which in turn means, hopefully, better performance. Life was very rosy for both the hardware community and the software community. On the hardware side, faster processors with speculative execution, superscalar capabilities, simultaneous multithreading, etc., were coupled with better process technology and higher frequency, which produced faster and faster processors. On the software side, you could write your program and expect it to get faster with every new generation of processors with any effort on your part! Until everything stopped around 2004. What happened?

Around 2004 Dennard scaling stopped. In 1974 Robert Dennard and several other authors [Dennard et al. 1974] published a paper that predicted that voltage and current should be proportional to the linear dimensions of the transistors. This has been known as *Dennard scaling*. It works quite well with Moore's law. Transistors get smaller and hence faster and their voltage and current also scale down, so power can stay almost constant, or at least will not increase fast. However, a closer look at the Dennard scaling prediction shows that the authors ignored leakage current (was very insignificant at the time when the paper was published). Now as transistors get smaller and smaller, leakage becomes more significant. The aforementioned paper also ignored the threshold voltage at which the transistor switches. Around 2004 those two factors overcame the prediction of Dennard scaling, and now we increase the number of transistors per Moore's law, but the power density also increases. Power density has many effects. One of them is that it increases packaging cost. Also, dealing with power dissipation becomes problematic and expensive. Given all that and given that dynamic power is proportional to clock frequency, we are stuck! What is the solution?

The solution is to stop increasing the clock frequency and instead increase the number of cores per chip, mostly at lower frequency. We can no longer increase frequency, otherwise power density becomes unbearable. With simpler cores and lower frequency, we reduce power dissipation and consumption. With multiple cores, we *hope* to maintain higher performance. Figure 1.1 [Rupp 2018] tells the whole story and shows the trends of several aspects of microprocessors throughout

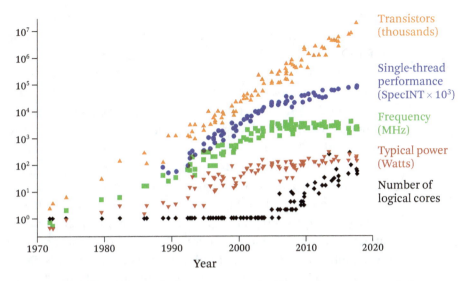

Figure 1.1   Trend of different aspects of microprocessors. (Karl Rupp. 2018. 42 years of microprocessor trend data. Courtesy of Karl Rupp https://github.com/karlrupp/microprocessor-trend-data; last accessed March 2018)

the years. As the figure shows, from around 2004 the number of logical cores started to increase beyond single core. The word *logical* includes physical cores with simultaneous multithreading (SMT) capability, also known as hyperthreading technology [Tullsen et al. 1995, Lo et al. 1997]. So a single core with four-way hyperthreading is counted as four logical cores. With SMT and the increase in the number of physical cores, we can see a sharp increase in the number of logical cores (note the logarithmic scale). If we look at the power metric, the 1990s was not a very friendly decade in terms of power. We see a steady increase. After we moved to multicore, things slowed down a bit due to the multicore era as well as the rise of dark-silicon techniques [Allred et al. 2012, Bose 2013, Esmaeilzadeh et al. 2011] and some VLSI tricks. "Dark silicon" refers to the parts of the processor that must not be turned off (hence dark) in order for the heat generated not to exceed the maximum capability that the cooling system can dissipate (called *thermal design point*, or TDP). How to manage dark silicon while trying to increase performance? This is the question that has resulted in many research papers in the second decade of the twenty-first century. We can think of the dark-silicon strategy as a way to continue increasing the number of cores per chip while keeping the power and temperature at a manageable level. The figure also shows that we stopped, or substantially slowed, increasing clock frequency. With this bag of tricks, we sustained, so far, a steady increase of transistors, as the figure shows at its top curve. There is one interesting curve remaining in the figure: the single thread (i.e., sequential programs) performance. There is a steady increase in single thread performance almost till 2010. The major reason is Moore's law, which allowed computer architects to make use of these transistors to add more features (from pipelining to superscalar to speculative execution, etc.). Another reason is the increase in clock frequency that was maintained till around 2004. There are some minor factors that make single thread performance a bit better with multicore. One of them is that the single thread program has a higher chance of executing on a core by itself without sharing resources with another program. The other is that of thread migration. If a single thread program is running on a core and that core becomes warm, the frequency and voltage will be scaled down, slowing down the program. If the program is running on a multicore, and thread migration is supported, the program may migrate to another core, losing some performance in the migration process but continuing at full speed afterwards.

The story outlined above relates the hardware tricks developed to manage the power and temperature near the end of Moore's law and the end of Dennard scaling. Those tricks gave some relief to the hardware community but started a very difficult problem for software folks.

Now that we have multicore processors all over the place, single thread programs are no longer an option.

The free lunch is over [Sutter 2005]! In the good old days, you could write a sequential program and expect that your program would become faster with every new generation of processors. Now, unless you write parallel code, don't expect to get that much of a performance boost anymore. Take another look at the single thread performance in Figure 1.1. We moved from single core to multicore not because the software community was ready for concurrency but because the hardware community could not afford to neglect the power issue. The problem is getting even harder because this multicore or parallel machine is no longer homogeneous. You are not writing code for a machine that consists of similar computing nodes but different ones. So now we need heterogeneous parallel programming.

We saw how we moved from single core to multiple homogeneous cores. How did heterogeneity arise? It is again a question of power, as we will see. But before we go deeper into heterogeneity, it is useful to categorize it into two types from a programmer's perspective.

A machine is as useful as the programs written for it. So let's look at heterogeneity from a programmer's perspective. There is this heterogeneity that is beyond a programmer's control. Surprisingly, this type has been around for several years now; and many programmers don't know it exists! There is also heterogeneity within a programmer's control. What is the difference? And how come we have been dealing with heterogeneity without knowing it?

1.2 Heterogeneity beyond Our Control

Multicore processors have been around now for more than a decade, and a lot of programs were written for them using different parallel programming paradigms and languages. However, almost everybody thinks they are writing programs for a heterogeneous machine, unless of course there is an explicit accelerator like a GPU or FPGA involved. In this section we show that we have not been programming a pure homogeneous machine even if we thought so!

1.2.1 Process Technology

Everybody, software programmers included, knows that we are using CMOS electronics in our design of digital circuits, and to put them on integrated circuits we use process technology that is based on silicon. This has been the norm for decades. This is true. But even in process technology, there is heterogeneity.

Instead of silicon, semiconductor manufacturing uses a silicon-insulator-silicon structure. The main reason for using silicon on insulator (SOI) is to reduce device capacitance. This capacitance causes the circuit elements to behave in nonideal ways. SOI reduces this capacitance and hence results in performance enhancement.

Instead of traditional CMOS transistors, many manufacturers use what is called a Fin field-effect (FinFET) transistor. Without going into a lot of electronics details, a transistor, which is the main building block of processors, is composed of gate, drain, and source. Depending on the voltage at gate, the current flows from source to drain or is cut off. Switching speed (i.e., from on to off) affects the overall performance. FinFET transistors are found to have a much higher switching time than traditional CMOS technology. An example of a FinFET transistor is Intel's tri-gate transistor, which was used in 2012 in the Ivy Bridge CPU.

Those small details are usually not known, or not well known, to the software community, making it harder to reason about the expected performance of a chip, or, even worse, of several chips in a multisocket system (i.e., several processors sharing the memory).

1.2.2 Voltage and Frequency

The dynamic power consumed and dissipated by the digital circuits of all our processors is defined by this equation: $P = C \times V_{cc}^2 \times F \times N$, where C is the capacitance, V_{cc} is the supply voltage, F is the frequency, and N is the number of bits switching. As we can see, there is a cubic relationship between the dynamic power and supply voltage and frequency. Reducing the frequency and reducing the supply voltage (up to a limit to avoid switching error) greatly reduces the dynamic power, at the expense of performance.

There are many layers in the computing stack that do dynamic voltage and frequency scaling (DVFS). It is done at the hardware level and per core. This means that even if we think we are writing an application for a homogeneous multicore, it is actually heterogeneous because it may have different performance measurements based on the processes running on each core. It is also done at the operating system (OS) level. With Intel processors, for example, the OS requests a particular level of performance, known as performance-level (P-level), from the processor. The processor then uses DVFS to try to meet the requested P-state. Up to that point, the programmer has no control and all this is happening under the hood. There are some techniques that involve application-directed DVFS. The programmer knows best when high performance is needed and when the program can tolerate lower performance for better power saving. However, this direction from the application can be overridden by the OS or the hardware.

1.2.3 Memory System

Beginning programmers see the memory as just a big array that is, usually, byte addressable. As programmers gain more knowledge, the concept of virtual memory will arise and they will know that each process has its known virtual address space that is mapped to physical memory that they see as a big array that is, usually, byte addressable! Depending on the background of the programmers, the concept of cache memory may be known to them. But what programmers usually do not know is that the access time for the memory system and large caches is no longer fixed. To overcome complexity and power dissipation, both memory and large caches are divided into banks. Depending on the address accessed, the bank may be near, or far, from the requesting core, resulting in nonuniform memory access (NUMA for memory) [Braithwaite et al. 2012] and nonuniform cache access (NUCA for cache) [Chishti et al. 2003]. This is one of the results from *heterogeneous* performance of memory hierarchy.

Another factor that contributes to the heterogeneity in memory systems is the cache hits and misses. Professional programmers, and optimizing compilers to some extent, know how to write cache-friendly code. However, the multiprogramming environment, where several processes are running simultaneously, the virtual memory system, and nondeterminism in parallel code make the memory hierarchy response time almost unpredictable. And this is a kind of temporal heterogeneity.

Another form of heterogeneity in memory systems is the technology. In the last several decades, the de facto technology used in memory hierarchy is dynamic RAM (DRAM) for the system memory, and in the last decade embedded DRAM or eDRAM for last-level cache, for some processors, especially IBM POWER processors. For the cache hierarchy static RAM (SRAM) is the main choice. DRAM has higher density but higher latency, due to its refresh cycle. Despite many architecture tricks, DRAM is becoming a limiting factor for performance. This does not mean it will disappear from machines, at least not very soon, but it will need to be complemented with something else. SRAM has shorter latency and lower density. This is why it is used with caches that need to be fast but not as big as the main system memory. Caches are also a big source of static power dissipation, especially leakage [Zhang et al. 2005]. With more cores on chip and with larger datasets, the big-data era, we need larger caches and bigger memory. But DRAM and SRAM are giving us diminishing returns from different angles: size, access latency, and power dissipation/consumption. A new technology is needed, and this adds a third element of heterogeneity.

The last few years have seen several emerging technologies that are candidates for caches and system memory. These technologies have the high density of DRAM, the low latency of SRAM, and, on top of that, they are nonvolatile [Boukhobza et al. 2017]. These technologies are not yet mainstream, but some of them are very close, waiting to solve some challenges related to cost, power, and data consistency.

Table 1.1 shows a comparison between the current (volatile) memory technologies used for caches and main memory, namely, DRAM and SRAM, and the new nonvolatile memory (NVM) technologies. The numbers in the table are approximate and collected from different sources but for the most part are from Boukhobza et al. [2017]. Many of the nonvolatile memory technologies have much higher density than DRAM and SRAM; look at the cell size. They also have comparable read latency and even lower read power in most cases. There are several challenges in using NVM that need to be solved and are shown in the table. For instance, write endurance is much lower than DRAM and SRAM, which causes a reliability problem. The power needed for write is relatively high in NVM. Consistency is also a big issue. When there is a power outage, we know that the data in DRAM and SRAM are gone. But for NVM when do not know whether the data stored are stale or updated. The power may have gone off while in the middle of a data update. A lot of research is needed to address these challenges. NVM can be used in the memory hierarchy at a level by itself, for example, as a last-level-cache (LLC) or in main memory, which is a vertical integration. NVM can also be used in tandem with traditional DRAM or SRAM, which is a horizontal integration. The integration of NVM in the memory

Table 1.1   **Comparison of several memory technologies**

	DRAM	SRAM	ReRAM	FeRAM	PCM	MRAM
Cell Size (F^2)	60–100	120–200	4–10	6–40	6–12	16–40
Endurance	10^{16}	10^{16}	10^9	10^{15}	10^{10}	$> 10^{15}$
Read Latency (ns)	30	1–100	10	20–80	20–50	3–20
Read Power	M	L	L	L	M	L
Write Latency (ns)	50	1–100	50	50	50	3–20
Write Power	M	L	H	H	H	H

hierarchy can be managed by the hardware, managed by the operating system, or left to the programmer to decide where to place the data. The first two cases are beyond the programmer's control. In the near future, memory hierarchy is expected to include volatile and nonvolatile memories, adding to the heterogeneity of the memory system.

Figure 1.2 shows a summary of the factors that we have just discussed.

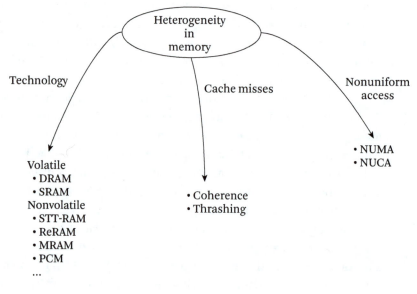

Figure 1.2   Factors introducing heterogeneity in memory.

1.3 Heterogeneity within Our Control

In the previous section we explored what happens under the hood that makes the system heterogeneous in nature. In this section we explore factors that are under our control and make us use the heterogeneity of the system. There is a big debate on how much control to give the programmer. The more control the better the performance and power efficiency we may get, depending of course on the expertise of the programmer, and the less the productivity. We discuss this issue later in the book. For this section we explore, from a programmer perspective, what we can control.

1.3.1 The Algorithm and The Language

When you want to solve a program, you can find several algorithms for that. For instance, look at how many sorting algorithms we have. You decide which algorithm to pick. We have to be very careful here. In the good old days of sequential programming, our main issues were the big-O notation. This means we need to optimize for the amount of computations done. In parallel computing, computation is no longer the most expensive operation. Communication among computing nodes (or cores) and memory access are more expensive than computation. Therefore, it is sometimes wiser to pick a worse algorithm in terms of computation if it has a better communication pattern (i.e., less communication) and a better memory access pattern (i.e., locality). You can even find some algorithms with the same big-O, but one of them is an order of magnitude slower than the other.

Once you pick your algorithm, or set of algorithms in the case of more sophisticated applications, you need to translate it to a program using one of the many parallel programming languages available (and counting!). Here also you are in control: which language to pick. There are several issues to take into account when picking a programming language for your project. The first is how suitable this language is for the algorithm at hand. Any language can implement anything. This applies to sequential and parallel languages. But some languages are much easier than others for some tasks. For example, if you want to count the number of times a specific pattern of characters appears in a text file, you can write a C program to do it. But a small Perl or Python script will do the job in much fewer lines. If you want less control but higher productivity, you can pick some languages with a higher level of abstraction (like Java, Scala, Python, etc.) or application-specific languages. On the other hand, the brave souls who are using PThreads, OpenMP, OpenCL, CUDA, etc., have more control yet the programs are more sophisticated.

Algorithm 1.1   **AX = Y: Matrix-Vector Multiplication**

for i = 0 **to** m − 1 **do**
   y[i] = 0;
   for j = 0 **to** n − 1 **do**
      y[i] += A[i][j] * X[j];
   end for
end for

1.3.2   The Computing Nodes

When you pick an algorithm and a programming language, you already have in mind the type of computing nodes you will be using. A program, or part of a program, can have data parallelism (single thread–multiple data), so it is a good fit for graphics processing units (GPUs). Algorithm 1.1 shows a matrix ($m \times n$) vector multiplication, which is a textbook definition of data parallelism. As a programmer, you may decide to execute it on a GPU or a traditional multicore. Your decision depends on the amount of parallelism available; in our case, it is the matrix dimension. If the amount of parallelism is not very big, it will not overcome the overhead of moving the data from the main memory to the GPU memory or the overhead of the GPU accessing the main memory (if your GPU and runtime supports that). You are in control.

If you have an application that needs to handle a vast amount of streaming data, like real-time network packet analysis, you may decide to use a field-programmable gate array (FPGA).

With a heterogeneous computing system, you have control of which computing node to choose for each part of your parallel application. You may decide not to use this control and use a high-abstraction language or workflow that does this assignment on your behalf for the sake of productivity—your productivity. However, in many cases an automated tool does not produce better results than a human expert, at least so far.

1.3.3   The Cores in Multicore

Let's assume that you decided to run your application on a multicore processor. You have another level of control: to decide which thread (or process) to assign to which core. In many parallel programming languages, programmers are not even aware that they have this control. For example, in OpenMP there is something called *thread affinity* that allows the programmer to decide how threads are assigned to cores (and sockets in the case of a multisocket system). This is done by setting some environment variables. If you use PThreads, there are APIs that help you assign thread to cores, such as pthread_setaffinity_np().

Not all the languages allow you this control, though. If you are writing in CUDA, for example, you cannot guarantee which streaming multiprocessor (SM)—which is a group of execution units in NVIDIA parlance—your block of threads will execute on. But remember, you have the choice to pick the programming language you want. So, if you want this control, you can pick a language that allows you to have it. You have to keep in mind, though, that sometimes your thread assignments may be overridden by the OS or the hardware for different reasons, such as thread migration due to temperature, high overhead on the machine from other programs running concurrently with yours, etc.

1.4 Seems Like Part of a Solution to Exascale Computing

If we look at the list of the top 500 supercomputers in the world,[1] we realize that we are in the petascale era. That is, the peak performance that such a machine can reach is on the order of 10^{15} floating point operations per second (FLOPS). This list is updated twice a year. Figure 1.3 shows the top four supercomputers. Rmax is the maximal achieved performance, while Rpeak is the theoretical peak (assuming zero-cost communication, etc.). The holy grail of high-performance computing is to have an exascale machine by the year 2021. That deadline has been a moving target: from 2015 to 2018 and now 2021. What is hard about that? We can build an exascale machine, that is, on the order of 10^{18} FLOPS by connecting, say, a thousand petascale machines with high-speed interconnection, right? Wrong! If you build the machine in the way we just mentioned, it would require about 50% of the power generated by the Hoover Dam! It is the problem of power again. The goal set by the US Department of Energy (2013) for an exascale machine is to have one exascale for 20–30 MW of power. This makes the problem very challenging.

Heterogeneity is one step toward the solution. Some GPUs may dissipate power more than multicore processors. But if a program is written in a GPU-friendly way and optimized for the GPU at hand, you get orders of magnitude speedup over a multicore, which makes the GPU better than a multicore in performance-per-watt measurement. If we assume the power budget to be fixed to, say, 30 MW, then using the right chips for the application at hand gets you much higher performance. Of course heterogeneity alone will not solve the exascale challenge, but it is a necessary step.

---

1. https://www.top500.org/

Rank	System	Cores	Rmax (TFlop/s)	Rpeak (TFlop/s)	Power (kW)
1	Summit: IBM Power System AC922, IBM POWER9 22C 3.07 GHz, NVIDIA Volta GV100, Dual-rail Mellanox EDR Infiniband IBM, DOE/SC/Oak Ridge National Laboratory, United States	2,397,824	143,500.0	200,794.9	9,783
2	Sierra: IBM Power System S922LC, IBM POWER9 22C 3.1 GHz, NVIDIA Volta GV100, Dual-rail Mellanox EDR Infiniband IBM / NVIDIA / Mellanox, DOE/NNSA/LLNL, United States	1,572,480	94,640.0	125,712.0	7,438
3	Sunway TaihuLight: Sunway MPP, Sunway SW26010 260C 1.45 Ghz, Sunway (/system/178764), NRCPC National Supercomputing Center in Wuxi (/site/50623) China	10,649,600	93,014.6	125,435.9	15,371
4	Tianhe-2A (MilkyWay-2): TH-IVB-FEP Cluster, Intel Xeon E5-2692v2 12C 2.200 GHz, TH Express-2, Intel Xeon Phi 31S1P (/system/177999), NUDT National Super Computer Center in Guangzhou (/site/50365) China	3,120,000	33,862.7	54,902.4	17,808

Figure 1.3   Part of the TOP500 list of fastest supercomputers (as of November 2018). (Top 500 List. 2018. Top 500 List Super Computers (November 2018) Courtesy Jack Dongarra; Retrieved November 2018; https://www.top500.org/lists/2018/11/)

2

Different Players: Heterogeneity in Computing

In this chapter we take a closer look at the different computing nodes that can exist in a heterogeneous system. Computing nodes are the parts that do the computations, and computations are the main tasks of any program. Computing nodes are like programming languages. Each one can do any computation, but some are way more efficient in some type of computations than others, as we will see.

In 1966 Michael Flynn classified computations into four categories based on how instructions interact with data. The traditional sequential central processing unit (CPU) executes an instruction with its data, then another instruction with its data, and so on. In Flynn's classification, this computation is called single instruction–single data (SISD). You can execute the same instruction on different data. Think of multiplying each element of a matrix by a factor, for example. This is called single instruction–multiple data (SIMD). The other way around, we refer to the same data that go through different instructions as multiple instruction–single data (MISD). There are not many examples of MISD around. With some stretch we can call pipelining a special case of MISD. Redundant execution of instructions, for reliability reasons, can also be considered MISD. Finally, the most generic category is multiple instruction–multiple data (MIMD). There are some generalizations. For instance, if we execute the same set of instructions on different data, we can generalize SIMD to single thread (or single program)–multiple data (SPMD). One of the advantages of such classifications is to build hardware suitable for each category, or for categories that are used more often, as we will see in this chapter.

2.1 Multicore

The first player in a heterogeneity team is the multicore processor itself. Figure 2.1 shows a generic multicore processor. The de facto definition of a core now is a CPU and its two level-1 caches (one for instructions and the other for data). Below the L1 caches are different designs. One design has a shared L2 and L3 cache, where L3 is usually the last-level cache (LLC) before going off-chip. An L2 cache is physically distributed and logically shared to increase scalability with the number of cores. This makes the shared L2 cache a nonuniform cache access (NUCA), as we saw in the previous chapter. An LLC cache is also NUCA. This LLC is designed either in SRAM or embedded DRAM (eDRAM). POWER processors, from IBM, have eDRAM as an LLC. Another design has private L2 caches per core followed by a shared LLC. In some recent processors, but not in many, there is also an L4 shared cache; for example, Intel's Broadwell i7 processor has a 128 MB L4 cache implemented in eDRAM technology. After the cache hierarchy, we go off-chip to access the system memory. Currently, the vast majority of system memory is in DRAM, but as we saw earlier, nonvolatile memory technology (such as PCM, STTRAM, MRAM, ReRAM, etc.) will soon appear and will be used with and/or in place of DRAM and also in some cache levels.

When we consider programming a multicore processor, we need to take into account several factors. The first is the process technology used for fabrication. It determines the cost, the power density, and the speed of transistors. The second factor is the number of cores and whether they support simultaneous multithreading (SMT) [Tullsen et al. 1995], called *hyperthreading* technology in Intel lingo and *symmetrical multithreading* in AMD parlance. This is where a single core can serve more than one thread at the same time, sharing resources. So if the processor has four cores and each one has two-way SMT capability, then the OS will see your

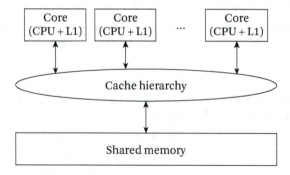

Figure 2.1   Generic multicore processors.

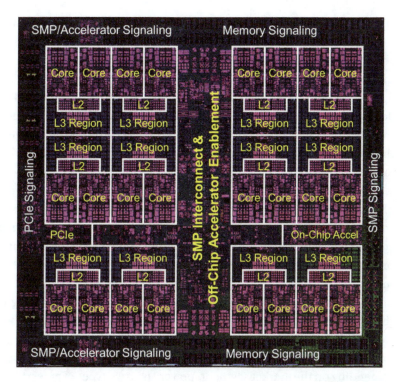

Figure 2.2 IBM POWER9 processor. (Courtesy of International Business Machines Corporation, © International Business Machines Corporation)

processor as one with eight cores. That number of cores (physical and logical) determines the amount of parallelism that you can get and hence the potential performance gain. The third factor is the architecture of the core itself as it affects the performance of a single thread. The fourth factor is the cache hierarchy: the number of cache levels, the specifics of each cache, the coherence protocol, the consistency model, etc. This factor is of crucial importance because going off-chip to access the memory is a very expensive operation. The cache hierarchy helps reduce those expensive trips, of course with help from the programmer, the compiler, and the OS. Finally, the last factor is scaling out. How efficient is a multisocket design? Can we scale even further to thousands of processors?

Let's see an example of a multicore. Figure 2.2 shows the POWER9 processor from IBM [Sadasivam et al. 2017]. The POWER9 is fabricated with 14 nm FinFET technology, with about eight billion transistors, which is a pretty advanced one, as of 2018, even though we see lower process technologies (e.g., 10 nm) but still very expensive and not yet in mass production. The figure shows 24 CPU cores. Each core can support up to four hardware threads (SMT). This means we can have up to 96 threads executed in parallel. There is another variation of the POWER9 (not shown in the figure) that has 12 cores, each of which supports up to 8 hardware threads, bringing the total again to 96 threads. The first variation, the one in the figure, has more physical cores so is better in terms of potential performance, depending on the application at hand, of course. Before we proceed, let's think from a programmer's perspective. Suppose you are writing a parallel program for this processor and the language you are using gives you the ability to assign threads (or processes) to cores. How will you decide which thread goes to which core? It is obvious that the first rule of thumb is to assign different threads to different physical cores. But there is a big chance that you have more threads than physical cores. In this case try to assign threads of different *personalities* to the same physical core; that is, a thread that is memory bound and a thread that is compute bound, or a thread with predominant floating point operations and one with predominant integer operations, and so on. Of course there is no magic recipe, but these are rules of thumb. Note that your assignment may be overridden by the language runtime, the OS, or the hardware. Now back to the Power9.

Each core includes its own L1 caches (instructions and data). The processor has a three-level cache hierarchy. L2 is a private 512 KB 8-way set-associative cache. Depending on the market segment, power9 has two types of cores: SMT4 and SMT8, where the latter has twice the fetch/decode capacity of the former. The L2 cache is private to SMT8, but if we use SMT4 cores, it is shared among two cores. Level 3 is shared, banked, and built out of eDRAM. But DRAM has high density, as we said earlier, and L3 is a massive 120 MB and has nonuniform cache access (NUCA). This cache is divided into 12 regions with 20-way set associativity per region. This means a region is local per SMT8 core, or two SMT4 cores, but can be accessed by the other cores with higher latency (hence NUCA). The on-chip bandwidth is 7 TB/s (tera bytes per second). If we leave the chip to access the main memory, POWER9 has a bandwidth of up to 120 GB/s to a DDR4 memory. These numbers are important because it gives you an indication of how slow/fast getting your data from the memory is, and how crucial it is to have a cache-friendly memory access pattern.

For big problem sizes, you will use a machine with several multicore processors and accelerators (like a GPU, for example). Therefore, it is important to know the bandwidth available to you from the processor to the accelerator because it affects your decision to outsource the problem to the accelerator or do it in-house in the multicore itself. POWER9 is equipped with PCIe (PCI Express) generation 4 with 48 lanes (a single lane gives about 1.9 GB/s), a 16 GB/s interface for connecting neighboring sockets, and a 25 GB/s interface that can be used by externally connected accelerators or I/O devices.

Multicore processors represent one of the pieces of the puzzle of heterogeneous computing. But there are some other chips that are much better than multicore processors for certain types of applications. The term *much better* here means they have a better performance per watt. One of these well-known chips that is playing a big role in our current era of artificial intelligence and big data is the graphics processing unit (GPU).

2.2 GPUs

Multicore processors are MIMD in Flynn's classification. MIMD is very generic and can implement all other types. But if we have an application that is single instruction (or program or thread)–multiple data, then a multicore processor may not be the best choice [Kang et al. 2011]. Why is that? Let's explain the reason with an example. Suppose we have the matrix-vector multiplication operation that we saw in the previous chapter (repeated here in Algorithm 2.1 for convenience). If we write this program in a multithreaded way and we execute it on a multicore processor, where each thread is responsible for calculating a subset of the vector Y, then *each* core must fetch/decode/issue instructions for threads, even though they are the same instructions for all the threads. This does not affect the correctness of the execution but is a waste of time and energy.

If we now try to execute the same program on a GPU, the situation will be different. SIMD architectures have several execution units (named differently by different companies) that share the same front end for fetching/decoding/issuing instructions, thus, amortizing the overhead of that part. This also will save a lot of the chip real estate for more execution units, resulting in much better performance.

Figure 2.3 shows a generic GPU. Each block that is labeled *lower level scheduling* can be seen as a front end and many execution units. Each execution unit is

Algorithm 2.1 **AX = Y: Matrix-vector multiplication**

for i = 0 to m − 1 do
    y[i] = 0;
    for j = 0 to n − 1 do
        y[i] += A[i][j] * X[j];
    end for
end for

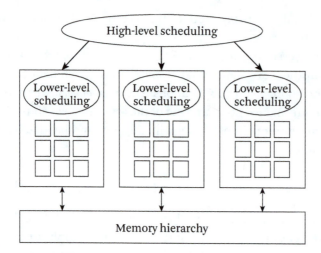

Figure 2.3   Generic GPU design.

responsible for calculating one or more elements for vector Y in the example of Algorithm 2.1. Why do we have several blocks then? There are several reasons. First, threads assigned to the different execution units within the same block can exchange data and synchronize among each other. It would be extremely expensive to do that among the execution units of all the chips as there are hundreds in small GPUs and thousands in high-end GPUs. So this distributed design makes the cost manageable. Second, it gives some flexibility. You can execute different SIMD-friendly applications on different blocks. This is why we have high-level scheduling shown in the figure. Execution units of different blocks can communicate, albeit in a slow manner, through the memory shared among all the blocks, labeled "memory hierarchy" in the figure, because in some designs there are some cache levels above the global memory as well as specialized memories like texture memory.

The confusing thing about GPUs is that each brand has its own naming convention. In NVIDIA parlance, those blocks are called streaming multiprocessors (SM or SMX in later version) and the execution units are called streaming processors (SPs) or CUDA cores. In AMD parlance, those blocks are called shader engines and the execution units are called compute units. In Intel parlance, the blocks are called slices (or subslices) and the execution units are just called: execution units. There are some very slight differences between each design, but the main idea is almost the same.

GPUs can be discrete, that is, stand-alone chips connected to the other processors using connections like PCIe or NVLink, or they can be embedded with the multicore processor in the same chip. On the one hand, the discrete ones are of course more powerful because they have more real estate. But they suffer from the communication overhead of sending the data back and forth between the GPU's memory and the system's memory [Jablin et al. 2011], even if the programmer sees a single virtual address space. On the other hand, the embedded GPUs, like Intel GPUs and many AMD APUs, are tightly coupled with the multicore and do not suffer from communication overhead. However, embedded GPUs have limited area because they share the chip with the processor and hence are weaker in terms of performance.

If you have a discrete GPU in your system, there is a high chance you also have an embedded GPU in your multicore chip, which means you can make use of a multicore processor, an embedded GPU, and a discrete GPU, which is a nice exercise of heterogeneous programming!

Let's see an example of a recent GPU: the Volta architecture V100 from NVIDIA [2017]. Figure 2.4 shows the block diagram of the V100. The giga thread engine at the top of the figure is what we called high-level scheduling in our generic GPU of Figure 2.3. Its main purpose is to schedule blocks to SMs. A block, in NVIDIA parlance, is a group of threads, doing the same operations on different data, assigned to the same SM, so that they can share data more easily and synchronize.

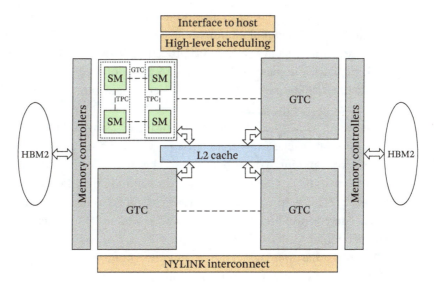

Figure 2.4 NVIDIA V100 GPU block diagram. (Based on NVIDIA, 2017. NVIDIA Tesla v100 GPU architecture)

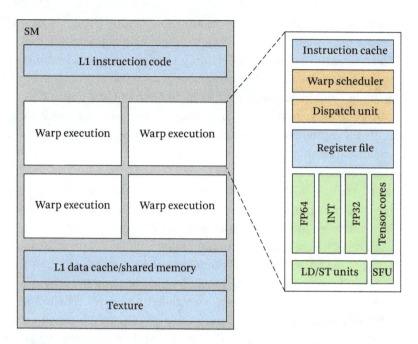

Figure 2.5   NVIDIA V100 GPU streaming multiprocessor. (Based on NVIDIA, 2017. NVIDIA Tesla v100 GPU architecture)

There is an L2 cache shared by all, and it is the last-level cache (LLC) before going off-chip to the GPU global memory, not shown in the figure. NVIDIA packs several SMs together in what are called GPU processing clusters (GPCs). In Volta there are six GPCs; each one has 14 SMs. You can think of a GPC as a small full-fledged GPU, with its SMs, raster engines, etc. The main players, who actually do the computations, are the SMs.

Figure 2.5 shows the internal configuration of a single SM. Each SM is equipped with an L1 data cache and a shared memory. The main difference is that the cache is totally transparent to the programmer. The shared memory is controllable by the programmer and can be used to share data among the block of threads assigned to that SM. This is why a block of threads assigned to the same SM can share data faster. There is also an L1 instruction cache and an L0 instruction cache for each warp scheduler. Warp? What is a warp?

Warp is a hardware concept transparent from the programmer, in theory! But in reality, when you write a program for such GPUs, you need to know about this concept to write a more efficient code. This is very similar to cache memory. People can write programs all their lives without knowing about the existence of caches. But if they know about them, they can write more efficient, cache-friendly code and therefore get better performance. You cannot always rely on the compiler to do the job for you because there is only so much that the compiler can do. Compilers will tend to be conservative. Moreover, the compiler will not pick the algorithm for you or change it. When it comes to parallel programming, compilers are not yet very mature, a problem that is even more noticeable with parallel programming for heterogeneous systems. Now back to the concept of warps: What is it? We said earlier that the different execution units in a GPU share the same front end, since it is single-thread–multiple data. This means that instructions are fetched/decoded, then all the execution units execute them, then more instructions are fetched/decoded, then the execution units execute them, etc. As you can see, the execution units are executing the instructions in *lock-step fashion*. No execution unit can proceed to the next instruction before all the execution units, connected to the same front end, finish this instruction. This is a price that has to be paid to amortize the cost of the front end over a large number of execution units. A *warp* is the set of threads that is executing the instructions in lock-step fashion. How many threads in a warp? Remember, it is a hardware concept, so if you say that the number of threads equals the number of threads in the block assigned to the SM, you would not be correct. The number of threads in a block is usually larger than the number of the execution units in an SM. Shall we make the number of threads in a warp equal the number of the execution units in an SM then? This is also not a very good decision, but the number, and type, of execution units changes from generation to generation, and we need to keep the warp size fixed to make compilation, scheduling, and execution easier. NVIDIA fixed the warp size to 32 threads. That number has been fixed across generations of GPUs. So a block of threads assigned to SMs is divided into a group of warps, and each warp is scheduled for execution. We can see from Figure 2.5 that each SM has four warp schedulers, which allows four warps to execute simultaneously. We said earlier that a programmer will benefit a lot from knowing about the concept of warps. Why? First, you can decide on the size of your blocks to be divisible by 32, hence making the best use of the available hardware. Second, if you know about warps, you will be very careful when writing a code with if-else conditions. As we said, threads in the same warp execute in lockstep fashion. What if there is an if-else and some threads have a true condition and others have false? In that case some threads execute the if part while the others wait. Then the other threads of the warp execute the else part while the first group waits. This means there is some kind of serialization here, reducing the parallelism and negatively affecting the performance. This issue is called *thread* or *branch diversion* [Vaidya et al. 2013], and people who write in CUDA, for instance, and are aware of the concept of warps are quite familiar with it. There is no magical solution for branch diversion. But there is a lot of work in the literature, both hardware solutions and software solutions, to reduce the negative effect of it [Han and Abdelrahman 2011]. A programming tip is to try to make all the threads in a warp have the same condition result (true or false).

After the warps have been scheduled for execution, the job of the execution units starts. As we see from Figure 2.5, there are several types of execution units in Volta: integer units, single-precision floating point units, double-precision floating point units, and tensor units. The tensor units are included in recent GPUs to accelerate operations used in aritifical intelligence applications, especially deep learning. There are also some special function units (SFUs) for specialized functions like sin(), cos(), etc.

All these SMs, with all their execution units, need to be fed with data on a continuous basis, and this is the job of the GPU global memory. This global memory has been fabricated, till now, using DRAM technology and optimized for bandwidth, unlike the main system memory that is optimized for latency. The global memory of the discrete GPUs in general suffers from two problems. The first is its low capacity compared to the system memory. If we look at GPU global memories, we see single-digit GB capacity until very recently. This small size increases the communication between the GPU memory and the system memory, which is the second problem of GPU global memory: communication overhead. Volta GPU uses a 3D stacked memory called high-bandwidth memory. Its size is 16 GB and it delivers 900 MB/s peak bandwidth. These two numbers from a state-of-the-art GPU illustrate the issues of capacity and communication.

From the above description, whenever you decide to outsource part(s) of your application to the GPU, you need to consider several things:

- Do I have data parallelism?
- How much communication is needed between system memory and GPU memory?
- Is the amount of data parallelism big enough to overcome the communication overhead?

If the answer is yes for all the above, then you will benefit from using GPUs if you can optimize your code to reduce the effect of branch divergence, make the best use of the available hardware, etc.

2.3 FPGA

Hardware and software are logically equivalent. What you can do with hardware you can do with software. The hardware implementation is much faster but not flexible and can be expensive in terms of price. Software implementation is very flexible but is slower because you have to execute it on general-purpose hardware that fetches, decodes, executes, etc. Can we have the flexibility of the software solutions with the performance of the hardware solutions but with less cost than an application-specific integrated circuit (ASIC)? FPGA comes very close to that [Hemsoth and Morgan 2017]. In very simple terms, FPGA is a hardware circuit that can be *reconfigured* by software. It can be updated even after it is deployed. That is, it can be configured while it is in the field, hence the first part of its name, *field*-programmable gate array. You can think of an FPGA as a group of logic gates (gate arrays) whose interconnection can be programmed, resulting in implementing different functions that can be as complicated as a soft processor. FPGAs are programmed using a hardware description language (HDL) such as Verilog or VHDL. Besides reconfigurability, FPGAs can scale by connecting several FPGA boards together, and they can efficiently handle a vast amount of streaming data.

So if your program has some parts that do not have data parallelism but are used frequently, then FPGAs can be a good option. One example of this is the Microsoft Catapult project [Caulfield et al. 2016] in which all Microsoft datacenters are FPGA equipped.

If you know the functions that you will use very frequently during execution, you can configure the FPGA before starting the execution. If you don't know these functions, of if these functions change during the lifetime of your application, then a profiling is needed, followed by reconfiguration, as shown in Figure 2.6. There is an overhead, of course, for profiling and for dynamically reconfiguring the FPGA during execution. But the performance boost obtained will overcome this overhead.

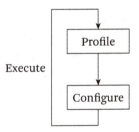

Figure 2.6 Dynamic reconfiguration of FPGA during execution.

There are many big players in the industry for designing FPGAs. Xilinx is one of them.[1] Intel, after it acquired Altera, is another one.[2]

2.4 Automata Processors

We saw that GPUs are good for data-parallel applications. FPGAs are good for streaming data and have the strength of flexibility in regard to hardware-implemented functions. There is another range of applications that have broad applicability: applications that depend on pattern-based algorithms. We can see these types of applications (pattern matching, pattern recognition, and so on) in many domains like data mining, bioinformatics, etc. [Wang et al. 2016]. Many of these domains depend on what we call *inexact matching*, which is computationally intensive and in which accuracy is often sacrificed for the sake of tractability. A few years ago, around 2012–2013, Micron Technology proposed a hardware chip that could natively implement nondeterministic finite automata (NFA), which is a mathematical tool for pattern matching and has less states than a deterministic finite automata (DFA) and hence can be efficiently implemented in hardware. Micron now has stopped development work for automata processing, but there are other researchers in academia (Center for Automata Processing at University of Virginia) and industry (Natural Intelligence Semiconductor Inc.) working on it.

NFA can have several active states at the same time. In real-life applications, active states can number in the hundreds, or even thousands. This means using a traditional multicore processor, with at most tens of cores, is not the best route to take. Using GPUs may be better but will suffer from a severe memory bandwidth bottleneck because each active state needs to be processed in a different memory location; states are usually presented as state-tables with every state containing information about the next state, resulting in a very cache-unfriendly access pattern. To have only one active state, we need to use DFA, with a booming number of states in comparison to NFA. This is where an automata processor (AP) comes in handy. Simply speaking, AP is a native implementation of NFA.

AP initial design depends on the inherent parallelism in memory. Memory can be seen as a matrix of rows and columns accessed with row addresses and column addresses. AP uses an 8-bit symbol as input to a row decoder. The decoder enables one out of 256 rows. Each column is represented by a state transition element (STE). The initial design has 49,152 columns (i.e, states). A subset of these states is

---

1. https://www.xilinx.com/products/silicon-devices/soc/zynq-ultrascale-mpsoc.html
2. https://www.intel.com/content/www/us/en/products/programmable/fpga.html

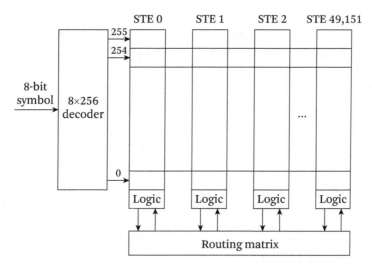

Figure 2.7   An automata processor chip (STE = state transition element).

active at any point of time. When a row is selected, the active states pass through a logic that can then activate another set of states using a reconfigurable routing matrix, as shown in Figure 2.7. To add versatility, AP is also equipped with logic elements that can implement AND, OR, NOT, NAND, or NOR gates. This helps with implementing combinational circuits of arbitrary complexity. Also, there are counter elements that can be configured to send an activation signal after the count reaches a threshold. An AP board has a set of AP chips.

Using the AP is very similar to any accelerator. The CPU configures the AP, offloads the data and program, then retrieves the result. There is a software development kit (SDK) for programming the AP with binding to languages like C and Python. The programming is done using a markup language called Automata Network Markup Language (ANML). ANML is used to describe the network. The binding to other languages, through the SDK, helps with describing automata networks, creating input streams, parsing output, and managing computational tasks.

2.5 Neuromorphic Chips

Everybody agrees that the brain is the most sophisticated, efficient, and powerful information processor in the universe, at least the part of the universe known to us. This pushes a lot of researchers to learn from Mother Nature, and we start to hear statements like *brain-inspired machines*, *cognitive computing* [Modha et al. 2011], etc. There are three types of relationships between the brain and computers.

The first is to simulate the brain on traditional (super)computers. In this case we are building tools for neuroscientists, medical doctors, etc. This is a traditional case of scientific computing. The second type is brain-machine interface, which has its (future) applications in many fields. The third type is to learn from how the brain works and use this experience to build better machines. This is what we are interested in for this section.

Neural networks in general have been around for several decades. Deep learning has been around for two decades with many advances enabled by the fact that hardware is becoming more and more powerful. Here we have to be very specific: we are getting inspired by the brain, but we are not building a brain. We are building a useful chip. So we have to be careful about what exactly we are getting inspired by [Zahran 2016]. For instance, we forget. Do we want machines that forget? We remember things in an approximate way. Is that what we want [Grigorian et al. 2015]? The design space is vast and open to possibilities [Potter 2001]. But for now the closest chips to the market are *neuromorphic chips*. These chips mimic neural networks, with several variations. Devices like memristors are used to model synapses of neural networks in neuromorphic chips [Sayyaparaju et al. 2017]. Neuromorphic chips are used in pattern matching, recognition, etc., after a phase of learning. However, we can say that neuromorphic chips are still not mainstream, but there is definitely a lot of progress.

2.6 Other Accelerators

Besides the chips that we have discussed in the previous sections, there are some special chips that are used, or can be used, in heterogeneous systems. Simply speaking, you can use any application-specific computing unit in a heterogeneous system setup; for example:

Digital signal processors (DSPs).   Processing analog signals, such as audio and video, is a must in today's environment. The main characteristic of such workloads is that they apply several mathematical equations on a stream of signals that are sampled. As with any specialized circuits, DSPs are more power efficient than general-purpose processors for these types of applications. This is why we see them a lot in many portable devices (smartphones, tablets, etc.). However, they can also be used in high-performance computing for some types of scientific applications when needed.

Quantum computing (QC).   QC has made very big steps forward, leading to advances that have gotten them close to production. Quantum computers do not depend on the traditional binary bits we use in our digital transistor-based computers. QC depends on quantum bits (qubits). Each qubit can be either zero, one, or something in between. Qubits can also exist in superposition and have two values at the same time. Quantum mechanics is mind boggling in itself when we consider concepts like entanglement and superposition! When we use these concepts to build a computing platform, things will be . . . well . . . mind boggling! A few years ago, quantum computing was considered more or less science fiction or a research endeavor beyond our current technology and too risky to pursue. Nowadays we can see many implementations of quantum computers. There are many big players investing in QC, including but not limited to Microsoft,[3] IBM,[4] Google,[5] and Intel.[6] The reason for this enthusiasm is that QC can be much faster than traditional computers in some types of applications (e.g., factorization), once they reach supremacy level (believed to be about 50 qubits).

Tensor processing units (TPUs).   The TPU is Google's chip designed specifically to support AI applications, more specifically to accelerate neural networks used in machine learning [Jouppi et al. 2017]. The chip was announced by Google in 2016. The main idea of a TPU is to be efficient in the computation operation frequently used in neural networks (NNs). If we look closely at how a traditional NN works, it depends on many neurons, each one summing up the product of a signal from other neurons with the weight of the connection between that neighboring neuron and the current one. For example, if a neuron is connected to 10 other neurons, it has to do 10 multiplications, multiplying the signal from the neuron by the weight connecting that neuron to the one in question, then adding the results. This series of multiplications and additions has a nickname: matrix multiplication. Simply speaking, we need a piece of hardware that can do matrix multiplication efficiently. You may say that GPUs are already doing this efficiently. This is true, but TPUs are doing an extra step of simplifications. They are using quantization to transform floating points (32 bits for single-precision) to 8-bit integers. The main philosophy here is that you do not really need the high precision of floating points to implement activation of neural networks. TPUs are implemented,

---

3. https://www.microsoft.com/en-us/quantum/

4. https://www.research.ibm.com/ibm-q/

5. https://research.google.com/pubs/QuantumAI.html

6. https://newsroom.intel.com/press-kits/quantum-computing/

unlike most other processors, on complex instruction set computing (CISC), where complex instructions are used to control matrix multiplication units that constitute the core of TPUs.

TPU and QC may not be available to customers to buy, at least for now. However, customers and other companies can have access to them through the cloud. What we can see here is that the computing devices in a heterogeneous system may not use the same instruction set. This requires a radical change in how we design our development environment and ecosystem of libraries, compilers, assemblers, linkers, etc.

When building a heterogeneous system, there are several decisions that have to be made. First, what are the types of processing elements needed in the system? Second, how many of each type is needed? Third, how is the memory hierarchy managed? There is a compilation of several accelerator chips that may exist in some heterogeneous systems besides the famous one.[7] The problem is more complicated when we talk about big machines (supercomputers, datacenters, etc.). In the next section we look at these types of decisions but for single chips.

2.7 Mix-and-Match

There are many chips in the market that include heterogeneous computing elements, besides of course the heterogeneity in memory access time, etc., that we have discussed earlier in this book. In this section we look at some examples of these chips.

2.7.1 Intel Coffee Lake

Intel Coffee Lake is a code name for a design by Intel of its new multicore. It appears in many brands like the i3, i5, i7, and i9. This architecture was released in October 2017 and uses Intel refined 14 nm technology, which uses tri-gate transistors. We will take an example of a Coffee Lake CPU: the Core i7-8700K. The i7-8700K has six cores with two-way hyperthreading technology, making the hardware support 12 threads. The chip also has integrated graphics: the Intel GT2. The cores, the integrated graphics, and a system agent (for I/O and memory) are connected using a ring interconnect. Figure 2.8 shows the architecture of Intel Skylake, which is almost the same as the Coffee Lake. The i7-800K has six cores instead of the four cores in the i7-6700K (shown in the figure) and has embedded graphics of 9.5 instead of 9. The architecture is the same.

---

7. https://www.sigarch.org/a-brief-guide-of-xpu-for-ai-accelerators/

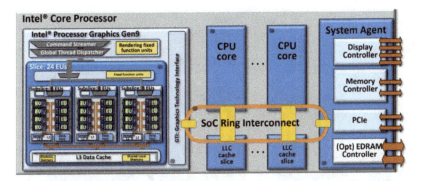

Figure 2.8   Intel architecture for the i7-6700K. (© Intel Corporation, Used with Permission)

The Intel GT2 is the generation 9.5 of Intel integrated graphics. The GT2 has one slice and 24 execution units. Let's take a quick look at the integrated graphics to see the difference between it and a discrete GPU similar to what we saw earlier in this book. One part of this embedded graphics unit is what is called the *unslice*. The unslice is the piece responsible for fixed-function media and geometry functions. It has its own power management and clock domain independent from other cores. This gives it the ability to turn off the slice or run it with higher performance on demand, saving power and optimizing performance. If we leave the fixed-function pipelines and move to a more *general-purpose execution* (yet GPU friendly), we find the slice. The slice is a cluster of subslices. Each sublice is a group of execution units. A global thread dispatch unit ensures load balancing among subslices. There is a difference between the execution units here and the CUDA cores, or SP, in NVIDIA discrete GPUs, for example. In the case of NVIDIA GPUs, each SP is an execution unit without a front end. So a group of threads, called a warp in NVIDIA parlance, executes in lockstep, hence SIMD (or STMD). In our case here, each execution unit is an independent unit. And each execution unit is sophisticated enough internally to be multithreaded, support seven threads, and execute instructions in SIMD fashion thanks to its support of 128 SIMD 32-bit registers per thread. By varying the number of execution units per subslice, the number of subslices per slice, and the number of slices, a different type of scalability serving different market segments can be built. Figure 2.9 shows the architecture of the embedded graphics. The embedded GPU hosts a slice of the L3 cache. Hence the GPU and the different cores in the chip share the L3 cache.

When it comes to memory hierarchy, each core has an IL1 (i.e., level 1 of instruction cache), a cache size of 32 KB, is 8-way set-associative, and it has 64 sets.

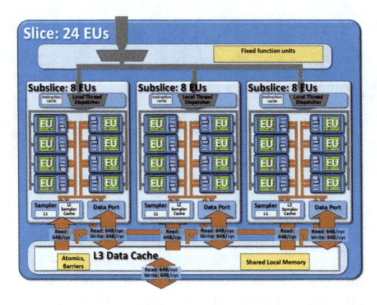

Figure 2.9 Embedded Intel graphics with one slice. (© Intel Corporation, Used with Permission)

The block has a size of 64 bytes across the whole cache hierarchy. This cache is shared by the two threads of the core. A DL1 cache (i.e., level 1 data cache) per core is also 32 KB and 8-way set-associative, with 64 sets. It uses a writeback policy to lower-level caches to reduce bandwidth requirements. The L2 cache is unified and noninclusive. It is 256 KB and 4-way set-associative, and also uses a writeback policy. L3 is the last-level cache. It is sliced, and each slice is up to 2 MB per core, but this cache is shared across all cores. The cache uses a writeback policy too.

2.7.2 Qualcomm Snapdragon 845

Our next example of a heterogeneous chip is a system-on-chip (SoC) targeting mobile platforms to support AI applications and virtual and augmented reality: Qualcomm's Snapdragon 845. The chip uses cores from Arm's Cortex-A75 (performance cores) and Cortex-A55 (efficiency cores) designs code-named Kryo-835. The cores use Arm's DynamIQ cluster technology, which enables the cores to share the cache hierarchy, as opposed to older designs where each of the cores have discrete hierarchies. The SoC also has the Adreno 600 series GPU. Because we are talking about SoC, the chip is *more heterogeneous* than traditional chips, as it has, besides the cores and the GPU, a DSP, a modem, and audio codec.

The performance cores have 256 KB private L2 caches while efficiency cores use 128 KB private L2 caches. The L3 cache is a shared 2 MB. In the memory controller, there is a 3 MB system cache that acts as an L4 cache shared by the whole SoC chip. But not all execution units share the memory hierarchy. There is an isolated island in that chip: the secure processing unit (SPU). The SPU has its own execution unit with its own random number generator and memory. It is important for the SPU to be isolated from the other pieces in order to defend against attacks.

This SoC is a very good example of the heterogeneity in hardware. Several different applications use the different execution units here. The development of a single application that leverages all the different heterogeneous execution units is still in progress, except in some areas of high-performance computing.

2.7.3 Arm big.LITTLE

In the past, designing CPUs for portable devices meant lower power consumption. But now, with the new wave of applications that need AI, augmented reality, etc., we also need high performance. High performance and low power seem to be mutually exclusive, but heterogeneity in hardware is a good step toward reconciling the two. For high performance, CPUs for portable devices need to provide the highest performance possible within the power envelope (remember, in portable devices there is no access to fans). For low performance, the CPU must consume very low power. These two requirements dictate the philosophy of Arm's big.LITTLE CPU.

As you may have guessed from its name, this chip uses two types of cores. Big processors are designed for highest performance. Little processors are designed for the lowest power consumption. The success of this architecture depends on assigning computing tasks to the core that are most suitable for it based on the required performance of that task. The task requirement can change several times in its lifetime. With cores with different capabilities, a task can migrate to the needed core during execution. Unused cores can be turned off. The two types of cores use Arm Cortex-A15 (for high performance) and A7 (for low power), hence the same Instructure Set Architecture (ISA). The high-performance core uses out-of-order execution with superscalar capability, while the low-performance core is a simple in-order core. Figure 2.10 shows a block diagram of the processor. GIC on the top is the global interrupt controller. Cache coherence is very much needed in this design to make task migration among cores as efficient as possible by keeping the data in caches coherent. Without it, migrating a task would require main memory access, which would result in a big performance loss.

As we said earlier, the performance efficiency depends on scheduling tasks to the right core at the right time. The big.LITTLE has two models of scheduling. The

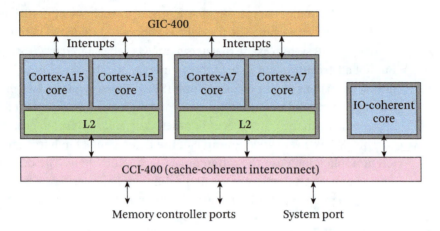

first one is called *CPU migration*. In this model, each big processor is paired with another little processor. This requires that the number of cores of each type must be equal. If we have four big cores and four little cores, the OS will see four cores. The task is assigned to one of the cores and moved between the big and the little based on its requirement using a variation of DVFS. The other model is called *global task scheduling*, which is the usual scheduling we expect. The OS sees all the cores and is aware of their different capabilities. Using heuristics, tasks are assigned to the most suitable cores. This second model does not require the processor to have the same number of cores of each type.

2.8   In Conclusion

In this chapter we looked at heterogeneity in computing. We had a tour of the different computing nodes and we saw some real-life examples. We saw heterogeneity across chips (discrete GPU, traditional multicore, FPGA, etc.). We also saw heterogeneity within the same chip. However, there is more to heterogeneity in hardware design. We need to look at the architecture from a different angle, which is the topic of the next chapter.

Architecture: Heterogeneity in Design

In the previous chapter we looked at the main pieces of the puzzle in a heterogeneous system: the computing nodes. In this chapter we put those pieces together and see the result of their interaction. The computing nodes need to access the memory, and storage, and need to be interconnected. So we look at the memory system as well as the interconnect. We also take a detailed look at some examples of supercomputers. Once we have a fully working system, we need to start worrying about two other factors that affect performance: security and bandwidth, which constitute the rest of this chapter.

3.1 Memory System

The memory system is actually a hierarchy, or many hierarchies for supercomputers, datacenters, hyperscalers, etc. The lowest level of this hierarchy, farthest from the processors, is the system memory. The higher levels are caches.

In the 1990s and the first decade of the twenty-first century, most of the research related to cache memory [Smith 1982] proceeded in two parallel paths. The first deals with caches for uniprocessor systems in an attempt to enhance one or more of the cache aspects, such as access time, accuracy, and power consumption. The second path deals with parallel architectures.

For uniprocessor systems, some work tries to capture the program behavior and adapt the cache based on this program's requirements [Calder et al. 1998, Dhodapkar and Smith 2002, Lee and Kim 2002]. Also, several proposals have been made in academia to enhance the memory system by dynamically varying one of its parameters [Peir et al. 1998, Kin et al. 1997, Veidenbaum et al. 1999, Albonesi 2002, Calder et al. 1996, Abella and Gonzalez 2006]. Improving the hit rate has been the main goal for a long time [Karkhanis and Smith 2002]; for instance, column-associative caches [Agarwal and Pudar 1993], filter caches [Kin et al. 1997], and predictive sequential-associative caches [Calder et al. 1996] are all geared toward increasing the hit rate by modifying the way an address is decoded and the sequence followed to find a block, at the expense of simplicity. Peir et al. [1996] proposed a path-balancing technique to help match the delays of caches and data paths. This has the effect of decreasing the access time. Another important aspect of a cache is its power consumption. Cache being one of the main power-hungry structures on-chip, it triggered a lot of research both in academia and industry [Flautner et al. 2002, Flautner et al. 2002, Ghose and Kamble 1999, Inoue et al. 2002, Kamble and Ghose 1997, Kaxiras et al. 2001, Kim et al. 2001, Kim et al. 2002, Kim et al. 2004a, Albonesi 2002]. For example, in Veidenbaum et al. [1999], the authors proposed a cache memory where cache line size is continuously adjusted by hardware based on observed application access.

The second path taken in memory system research is the cache hierarchy for multiprocessor systems. The research in that area consists mainly of coherence protocol schemes [Archibald and Baer 1986, Agarwal et al. 1988, Eggers and Katz 1989, Tomasevic and Milutinovic 1993, Moshovos 2005]. That path is now targeting multicore architectures [Hammond et al. 1997, Krishnan and Torrellas 1999, Cheng et al. 2006, Ekman et al. 2002, Nayfeh 1998].

These two paths in memory system research proceed in parallel. But with the introduction of multicore architectures (aka chip multiprocessors or CMPs), the two paths started to converge [Beckmann and Wood 2004], and the main theme was the high bandwidth available on-chip, as opposed to the limited, and more expensive, off-chip bandwidth. However, wire delay represents a big challenge because it does not scale with the transistor [Agarwal et al. 2004, Beckmann and Wood 2004]. This leads to the introduction of networks on-chip [Dally and Towles 2001, Benini and DeMicheli 2002, T. T. Ye 2003], which uses the experience gained at designing packet-switched networks to design on-chip networks that connect cores and caches. With the increase in the number of on-chip cores and the fact that most of the current designs still make use of the traditional design of a private L1 cache for each core and a shared L2 cache among cores, the problem of sharing the L2 caches among cores becomes important both in academia [Kim et al. 2004b, Qureshi and Patt 2006] and in industry. The problem of cache sharing for multicore architectures uses experience gained from cache partitioning in clustered architectures [Farkas et al. 1997]. Another trend is to use small caches to act as an aggregate large cache [Varadarajan et al. 2006, Chang and Sohi 2006]. These methods have the advantage of saving power but do not solve the problem of application interference in caches, where two applications have conflicting cache requirements, which happens very frequently in simultaneous multithreading architectures [Tullsen et al.

1995, Lo et al. 1997], multicore architectures [Sinharoy et al. 2005, Borkar et al. 2006, Ramanathan 2006, Broadcom Corporation 2006], and systems built as a hybrid of the two, like the Niagara (UltraSPARC T1) [Kongetira et al. 2005].

Another line of research that has been targeting single core and has migrated, without many enhancements or changes at first, to multicore is cache replacement policy [Jeong and Dubois 2003, Reineke et al. 2006, Guo and Solihin 2006, Megiddo and Modha 2004, Qureshi et al. 2006, Al-Zoubi et al. 2004, Wong and Baer 2000]. Cache replacement policy decides which block to evict to make room for a new incoming block.

Cache replacement starts to evolve with the widespread usage of multicore and manycore processors [Pekhimenko et al. 2015, Ros et al. 2015, Guo et al. 2013]. However, cache hierarchy nowadays needs to deal with different types of scenarios: heterogeneous multicore, like multicore with embedded GPUs, and many-core chips like GPUs [Xie et al. 2015].

Another aspect of the memory hierarchy is the inclusion property. It goes without saying that most hierarchies now do not support inclusion, except at the last-level cache. The main reason for that is to make the best use of the chip area. With inclusion, data is replicated in all the higher cache levels ("higher" means closer to the processor). As the number of cores increases, the data replication increases, especially when there is a lot of data sharing among cores. But if we do not have an inclusion property at the last-level cache, which is almost one big shared cache before going off-chip, then coherence will happen off-chip, which will result in very high performance degradation.

3.2 Interconnect

We are in the big-data era. Machines are number-crunching huge amounts of data. But in order to solve big and important problems, data have to be moved both in the memory hierarchy and among cores/processors. This makes the interconnect a vital part of overall performance in any system.

There are several aspects of interconnect in any system:

- The topology. What is the shape of interconnection among the different pieces? A piece can be a processor, a computing node, a switch, etc.

- The granularity. What are we connecting (cores, chips, full cabinets)?

- The technology. What is the material we are using (fiber optics, copper)? A single system can use different technologies at different granularity levels; that is, using copper to connect cores, fiber optics to connect processors, and so on.

- The protocol. How are data encoded as electrical or laser signals?

- The switching and routing technology. Data may have to be routed through several hops in order to go from one point to another point. How is this done?

The technology, protocol, and switching affect the bandwidth sustained by the interconnect and hence the overall performance of data movement. The granularity is just the playground of the interconnect. For example, connecting cores inside a chip [Kumar et al. 2005, Jerger et al. 2017] has different characteristics than connecting several cabinets. Inside the chip the distances are much shorter and the bandwidth is much higher, but space and power are more restrictive than off-chip and among cabinets. In this section we take a look at the different aspects of interconnect.

3.2.1 Topology

The topology is the shape of interconnection. In its general form, it is an undirected graph of connected vertices. These vertices can be cores, processors, routers, blades, cabinets, or anything we want to connect. Of course connecting all vertices to each other (i.e., a fully connected graph) is very expensive in terms of area and power consumption. Each connection consumes, and dissipates, power. At the same time, we want each node, a vertex in the graph, to be able to communicate with any other node. This is where topology comes in. It answers the question, What are the best and most economical interconnections among the nodes? Nodes exchange messages.

An interconnection network can be direct or indirect. Suppose we have N nodes to be interconnected. For direct networks, the nodes that need to be interconnected reside inside the network. Indirect networks have the nodes sitting outside the network. Both cases are shown in Figure 3.1. In the case of an indirect interconnect (Figure 3.1(a)), the interconnect itself is made of routers and switches, while in direct interconnect (Figure 3.1(b)), the node itself contains the router or switch.

The topology can have a regular shape (mesh, ring, torus, etc.) or an irregular one. How do we compare two different topologies? One of the important measurements is the diameter. For a message to go from node A to node B, if the two nodes are not directly connected, the message has to go through several hops (called the *routing distance*). The diameter is the maximum number of hops between any two nodes. The lower the diameter the better because then the message will travel less distance. Figure 3.2(a) shows a bus interconnect. The longest routing distance is two, which the distance needed to send a message from node A to node C. So the diameter of this topology is two. If we move to the ring interconnect in Figure 3.2(b),

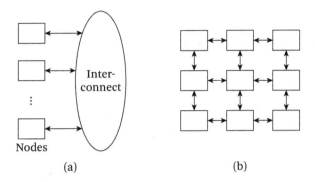

Figure 3.1 (a) Indirect interconnect; (b) direct interconnect.

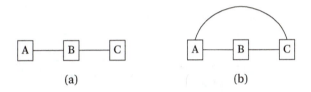

Figure 3.2 (a) Bus interconnect; (b) ring interconnect.

we can easily see that the diameter is now one, which is better. As you may have realized, the diameter grows with the number of nodes. Only a fully connected topology has a fixed diameter of one. A ring of *n* nodes has a diameter of floor (n/2).

Besides the ring and the bus, there are many different interconnect topologies. Figure 3.3 shows some examples. As you can see from the figure, some topologies are indirect interconnect (crossbar, tree, and omega) and some are direct interconnect (hypercube, mesh, and torus). Of course there are systems with irregular topology. The interconnect can be sophisticated to include contention control through routing, in which case messages sent from source to destination may take different routes depending on which links are heavily used.

That covers the topology. How about the technology used for the links?

3.2.2 Technology

The interconnect was designed mainly using copper from the old days until today. Let's take on-chip as an example. A link between two entities (core, cache, etc.) is a group of parallel copper wires. The more parallel wires we put, the higher the bandwidth we get because we can move more bits in parallel. But more parallel

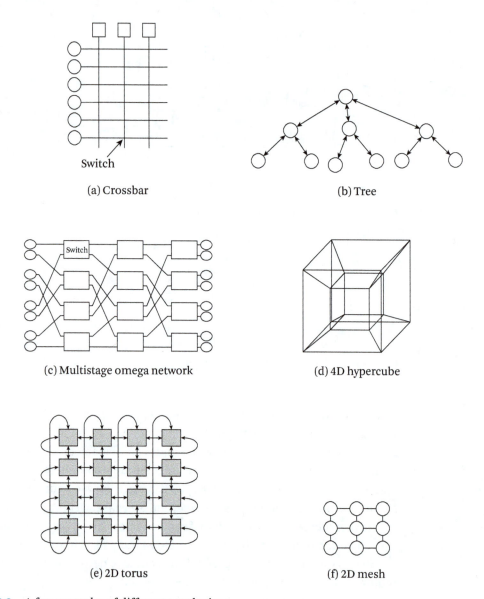

Figure 3.3 A few examples of different topologies.

wires means more chip area. If we don't have this needed area, then we can make each copper wire thinner. Thinner wire increases its resistance and hence its temperature and the power it dissipates. So we have a trade-off of bandwidth versus power. This trade-off is not the only problem we face. Wire delay is a performance bottleneck.

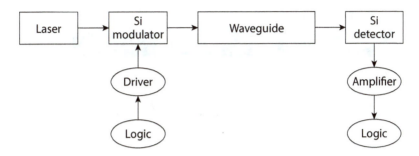

Figure 3.4 Generic setup for on-chip optical communication.

Moving data around from core to shared cache or among different banks of a cache affects performance in a negative way. The communication also affects programming. Programmers now need to manage data locality (to reduce data movement) and data communication (to move data in an efficient way). If there is a broadcast channel and it has low latency, then the programmer's task will be easier. This is where optical interconnection comes into play.

Using photonics, we have several advantages. The power consumption is less than copper. Contention is not a big problem because you can use different wavelengths. You can have arbitrary interconnection because two overlapping laser beams will not interfere. In Kurian et al. [2010], for example, the authors use nanophotonic technology to implement a fast, efficient global broadcast network implemented as a ring connecting all the cores on-chip. This network can be used together with a traditional point-to-point copper network. Optical interconnection is getting more and more momentum and is already in use on-board and across boards [Kobrinsky et. al. 2004, Kodi and Louri 2007, Xue et al. 2010, Nitta et al. 2013]. Figure 3.4 shows a typical optical interconnect that can be used on-chip. The main processor is of course electrical (the logic part). There must be a modulator to transform electrical pulses into a laser beam by modulating the laser beam using a driver. The modulated laser beam is directed, using a waveguide, to its destination where a detector returns it to its electrical form to be consumed by the logic. The main drawback for optical interconnection is that it is still more expensive than traditional copper interconnection.

As we can see, there is heterogeneity here too, because we can have optical and copper interconnect in the same system. Each network can have different topology too.

Now that we can have different topologies and different technologies, how are data sent across the interconnect links? There must be some kind of protocols.

Table 3.1 **Bandwidth provided by HT**

Version	Max. Aggregate Bidirectional Bandwidth (GB/s)
1.0	12.8
2.0	22.4
3.0	41.6
3.1	51.2

3.2.3 Protocol

In computer systems, data move from one entity to another. These data take the form of streams of bits, messages, packets, etc. (depending on how you look at it). How do these data move? There must be a protocol between sending and receiving partners, whether these partners are CPUs, cache banks, or even full cabinets. There have been many protocols in the last several decades. In this section we look at three of the most widely used protocols: HyperTransport, PCI Express (PCIe), and NVLink.

HyperTransport (HT)[1] is a point-to-point link connecting CPUs to one another and connecting CPUs to I/O devices. HT was first introduced by AMD in 2001 and has undergone several updates by many partners. It is a packet-based technology; that is, messages sent are divided into packets. Some packets are for control and management while the rest of the packets are for payload, and each packet is sent individually to its destination, where it is combined with the other packets to reconstruct the original message. This technology is used on-board and with switches and routers but not on-chip. Table 3.1 shows the maximum aggregate bandwidth that HT can provide at its maximum frequency.

PCIe, Peripheral Component Interface Express, is usually found on-board. It is a point-to-point serial interconnect that is packet based. PCIe link can range from one lane (x1) to 32 lanes (x32). Each lane consists of two wires, each of which is unidirectional. Table 3.2 shows the typical speed of each wire (i.e., way) in a lane. Some numbers are approximations. PCIe v4.0 is just out the door (in 2018) and v5.0 is still under development and revision.

NVLink was introduced by NVIDIA to connect GPUs to each other and to the CPU. Previously, GPUs were connected to the CPU using PCIe. But PCIe be-

---

1. https://www.hypertransport.org/

Table 3.2 Bandwidth provided by PCIe

Version	Bandwidth/Lane/Way (GB/s)
1.x	0.25
2.x	0.5
3.x	1
4.0	2
5.0	4

came a bottleneck for the high-bandwidth requirement of GPUs. This is why NVIDIA introduced NVLink. NVLink uses high-speed signaling interconnect (NVHS), which transmits data over differential pairs. Eight of these differential pairs form a sublink. Each sublink sends data in one direction. Two sublinks (each at different directions) form a link. This link can connect a CPU to a GPU or connect two GPUs. NVLink 1.0 has a total bandwidth of 160 GB/s while 2.0 has 300 GB/s.

3.2.4 Examples

We have seen examples of interconnect inside the chip and on-board. What about higher granularity? In this section we take a quick look at some interconnect at high granularity in supercomputers. The trend now is to use switches with more skinny ports (i.e., ports with fewer parallel bits) than fewer fatter ports. The main reason for that is that signaling rates—the electrical signals used to send the data— have gone up relative to the sizes of the network packets. This means the penalty for sending large packets through skinny ports (i.e., serialization) has gone down. Another trend is to have switches with more ports. These are called *high-radix* switches. The implication of this is that we can have network topology with lower diameter. Now, let's see some examples.

Cray Aries interconnect has a dragonfly topology. This is a hierarchical topology introduced in 2008 [Kim et al. 2008]. At the higher level, there are groups that are connected in an *all-to-all* link. This means each group has a direct link to every other group. The topology inside each group, the lower level, can be anything, as shown in Figure 3.5. This hierarchical organization comes in handy in supercomputers, for example, where we need to have interconnects at different levels (as we will see in the examples discussed in Section 3.3).

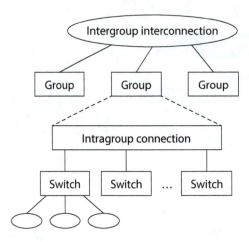

Figure 3.5   Dragonfly interconnect.

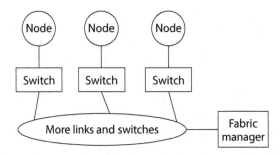

Figure 3.6   Intel Omni-Path interconnect.

The Aries router can support different interconnection technologies and protocols (PCIe, Optical, etc.).

Intel Omni-Path interconnect was built with three goals in mind: low latency, low power, and high throughput. Intel wants to use this technology for future exascale computing, so scalability must also be a goal. This interconnect has a fabric manager chip that sees the whole picture of the topology. The manager cooperates with the switches in the interconnect to decide on the best routes for each packet based on the congestion status. The main design is shown in Figure 3.6.

3.3 Examples of Supercomputers

In the previous chapter we looked at heterogeneity inside the chip. We saw examples of chips with heterogeneous computing nodes. This chapter goes a step further and we look at the whole system when we connect many computing nodes. As we did in the previous chapter, we look at examples of heterogeneous machines at the system level. Because we are discussing high-performance computers, the memory, at that high level, is distributed. The design philosophy for most of them is the same: few processors in a node (or card), several nodes in a blade, several blades in a cabinet, and then multiple cabinets. At each level there are interconnections. Processors in a node share memory. Once we are at the blade level, we have distributed memory. The naming (e.g., rack instead of blade) and number of levels may differ among companies, but this philosophy of design allows scalability and at different granularities when needed (adding more cards, blades, etc.). Figure 3.7 summarizes these concepts.

3.3.1 Cray XC50 Supercomputer

Our first example is the Cray XC50. The heterogeneity is obvious. It has two types of processing nodes: general purpose nodes (Cavium ThunderX2 Arm or Intel Xeon) and accelerator nodes. The accelerator node is an NVIDIA Tesla P100 (Pascal architecture) GPU. Each computing node has two processors, an Intel Xeon or Cavium Arm, and an NVIDIA P100. Every 4 nodes form a blade. Up to 16 blades

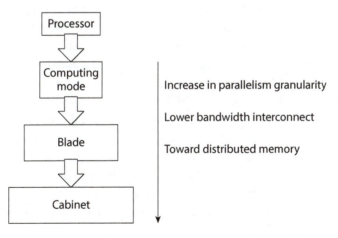

Figure 3.7   Design philosophy of a high-performance machine.

form a chassis. A cabinet can have up to three of these chassis and a claimed peak performance of 1 PFLOPS (peta floating point operations per second). By introducing Arm and Intel processors, CRAY made their machine very flexible to accommodate different host processors.

Each computing node has a one-to-one matching of a multicore (whether from Intel or Arm) and an accelerator. This makes for a balanced compute to accelerator ratio. This balance, coupled with a choice of CPU (Intel vs. Arm), allows Cray to cater to different heterogeneous workloads. Even though the memory is distributed across cards, the address space of general-purpose processors (i.e., the nonaccelerators) is extended to access all the physical memory in the system. This makes the machine programmable with languages like MPI and also with schemes of partitioned global address spaces (PGAS) like Unified Parallel C (UPC) and Fortran with Coarrays. This capability of allowing processors to access the physical address of the system is enabled through the Aries interconnect.

The Aries interconnect by Cray is a chip (router), a topology, an interconnect technology, and a protocol. There is an Aries chip in each computing node. In that protocol is a network address that consists of three parts: (1) an 18-bit node identifier, (2) a 12-bit memory domain handle associated with a memory segment registered at the remote node, and (3) a 40-bit offset into this segment. This makes a 70-bit address that allows a processor in a node to access all physical addresses in the system. At the technology front, the Aries interconnect uses optical connection, and for a good reason. The downside with small-diameter topologies is that the links (i.e., cables) are a bit long, for example, 15 meters. With that length, using copper interconnect becomes very slow. This is why Cray uses optical interconnect here. However, the optical interconnect is not used everywhere in that system but is used in tandem with copper wire, as we will see shortly. The topology used is called dragonfly. This topology has a very small diameter. There is an all-to-all link inside the chassis. This is done with copper wires because the length is short. Then there is another all-to-all link among six chassis. We saw earlier that every three chassis form a cabinet. So we have an all-to-all among the chassis forming two cabinets. At that level of chassis, the connections are done in copper too, for two reasons. The first is to reduce the cost of the system because optical interconnect is very expensive. The second is that the wires are short so copper wires will not hurt performance. Among groups of two cabinets we have optical cables and connections in an all-to-all topology because here the cable's length is high. That is, the connection between any two points does not need to go through many hops—actually, only two hops if the two nodes are in the same group of two cabinets, based on the description above—and it can get between any two nodes in the system with at most five hops.

3.3.2 Sunway TaihuLight Supercomputer

The Sunway TaihuLight supercomputer, developed at the National Research Center of Parallel Computer Engineering and Technology (NRCPC) in China, is the top-ranked supercomputer in the Top500 list of November 2017. This machine is built around the custom-designed Chinese 1.45 GHz SW26010 (ShenWei) processor. Each core supports one thread. The simplicity of the design makes it very efficient in providing high FLOPS. The core group is made up of 65 cores. One of these 65 cores is used for management and the rest for computations. Those computation cores are organized as an 8×8 grid. Every four core groups form a node. The core groups communicate through a network on-chip. A group of 256 nodes forms a supernode. Every four supernodes form a cabinet, and the whole system has 40 cabinets. This means these machines have over 10.6 million cores. The main design goal of the whole system is high efficiency in floating point operations. Its performance is 93 PFLOPS. There is an interconnect within each cabinet and another one to tie all the cabinets together. Those interconnects are custom developed but depend mostly on PCIe connections. The main drawback of that design is that the memory system is very slow. This is the price paid to get a very high GFLOPS/Watt relative to the other machines in the top 10 of the Top500 list. So computation is great but moving data is not.

You may wonder why we are using this machine as an example of a heterogeneous system even though it has one type of computing nodes. The heterogeneity here is very obvious in the interconnection: within a node, within a supernode, in a cabinet, and across cabinets. This makes data placement and movement challenging. Even though this supercomputer was the top of the Top500 list based on the LINPACK benchmark, the gold standard of HPC for over two decades that emphasizes floating point muscle, it did not show great performance for the HPCG benchmark, where the emphasis is more on data movement.

3.3.3 Titan Supercomputer

The Titan supercomputer, from Oak Ridge National Laboratory, is ranked fifth in the Top500 list. We can see the same design philosophy: processors to nodes to blades to cabinet. A node consists of a 16-core AMD Opteron processor and an NVIDIA Kepler GPU. The AMD processor is connected, through DDR3, to 32 GB of memory. The GPU is connected, through GDDR5, to 6 GB of memory. The CPU and GPU are connected with PCIe. Together all of these form a node. Every four nodes

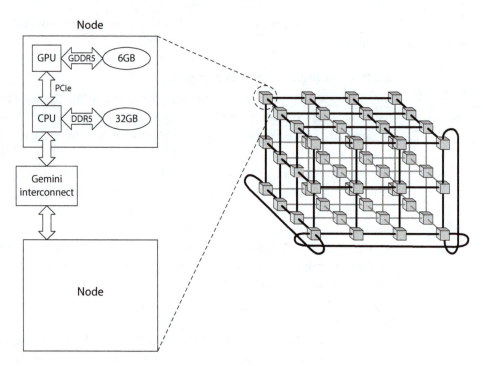

Figure 3.8   Main design of the Titan supercomputer.

form a blade. A cabinet has 24 blades. The system consists of 200 cabinets, making the total number of nodes 18,688. Every two nodes are connected to Cray's Gemini interconnect. This interconnect forms a 3D torus, as shown in Figure 3.8.

3.4 Security Challenges Facing Heterogeneous Computing

With the sophistication we have in modern machines in interconnect, processing nodes, memory systems, and storage, keeping these machines safe in this interconnected world is a challenge. Moreover, the amount, type, and speed of data to be processed are also becoming heterogeneous, complicating the problem of securing the whole system from cyberattacks.

In 2008, when an infected flash drive was inserted into one of the US Department of Defense (DoD) laptops, the DoD suffered a significant compromise of its classified military computer networks.[2] The Stuxnet attack exposed the inherent problems with computer-controlled systems in critical infrastructure and indus-

---

2. http://www.defense.gov/home/features/2010/0410 cybersec/lynn-article1.aspx.

trial process control systems.[3] This previously classified incident was the most significant breach of US military computers ever and marked a turning point in US cyber defense strategy. It was also a turning point in computer system research and industry to make security as important as performance and cost, not just an afterthought. The sensitive information and critical applications handled by computers makes building a trusted computer system a necessity and not a luxury. This is easier said than done due to the proliferation of methods by which a computer system can be attacked. Trusted computing is a paradigm that has emerged to address the security concerns in general-purpose computing systems [TCG 2008]. There are software-oriented and hardware-oriented ways to attack a system, and also software-oriented and hardware-oriented ways to add security to computer systems and build trusted platforms. To design a trusted computing system, security has to be systematically incorporated into the various stages during the design of such systems: including system architecture, hardware implementation, and software implementation [McGinn-Combs 2007].

Securing heterogeneous systems is even more challenging due to the different ways programs are executing in different accelerators and the need to move a lot of data around. Prior to execution, a program resides on the disk. When this program starts execution, it is copied to the system memory to be fetched and executed by the processor. This program can be tampered with while it is on the disk [Nijim et al. 2006, Hughes and Murray 2005, Ruan et al. 2009, Abualsamid 1998], on the bus from disk to memory or from memory to the processor [Su et al. 2009, Elbaz et al. 2005, Coburn et al. 2005], while in the memory [Di Crescenzo 2005, Yan et al. 2006, Vaslin et al. 2009], or when moving from node to node (or blade to blade or cabinet to cabinet in large systems). It can also be modified by malicious software [Lin 2008]. Simply using encryption and decryption schemes is not enough to ensure that programs will be secure, because side channel attacks can be extremely dangerous [Tiri 2007, Standaert et al. 2009, Wang et al. 2009].

Computer systems can be compromised using software attacks and/or hardware attacks [Waksman and Sethumadhavan 2010, Karri et al. 2010]. The most obvious threat model is time of check/time of use (TOCTOU) [Bratus et al. 2008], where there is an interval between the time the software has been checked for integrity and the time the software is used. During that interval, the software can be tampered with and illegitimately modified. Other types of attacks involve taking advantage of program vulnerabilities. Most programs usually contain vulnerabilities. Over the

---

3. http://www.globalpost.com/dispatch/asia/101016/stuxnet-cyber-warfare-computer-science.

years attackers have devised various ways to exploit vulnerabilities in programs and transfer control to their attack code. Some of the most common types of attacks are as follows:

Buffer overflow attacks [Cowan et al. 1998] arise due to lack of bounds checking on the size of the input array being stored in the buffer. Attackers make use of an unchecked buffer in a program and overwrite it with their own data, thus allowing unintended control transfer to their own attack code. This is also known as the "stack smashing attack" and is one of the highest reported vulnerabilities to CERT.[4] Several hardware-based solutions, like a secure return address stack [Lee et al. 2003], using a nonexecutable stack [Cowan et al. 1998], etc. have been proposed to thwart these attacks. Secure languages such as Cyclone, which perform array bounds checking, have also been proposed. As more and more applications are developed, buffer overflow attacks still form a major share of the vulnerabilities reported.

Return-into-libc [Nergal 2001] exploits buffer overflow to overwrite the return address with the address of a C library function such as `system()`. Instead of returning into code located in the stack, control is transferred to a memory area occupied by a dynamic library. Since it uses existing code rather than the attacker's shell code, a return-into-libc attack is very difficult to detect.

Code injection attacks [Kc et al. 2003] inject malicious code into a running application and then cause the injected code to be executed. The execution of the injected code allows the attacker to gain the privileges of the executing program. Instruction set randomization has been proposed to counter code injection attacks.

Replay attacks [Wheeler 2008] involve fraudulent repetition of valid data transmission by an attacker. If the destination does not detect the duplicate copies of the data being sent by the attacker, the attack is successful.

As we can see, for each type of attack there are many attempts to defend against it. This means if we want to protect our program from, say, 10 different attacks, we need to implement 10 different defenses! *A unified security system is needed to ensure program integrity against most, if not all, different threats.*

---

4. http://www.cert.org defines CERT as an organization devoted to ensuring that appropriate technology and systems management practices are used to resist attacks on networked systems and to limit damage and ensure continuity of critical services in spite of successful attacks, accidents, or failures. CERT is not an acronym.

On the hardware side, attacks can result from a malicious piece of hardware (called a *hardware Trojan*) inserted into the computer system [Waksman and Sethumadhavan 2010, Karri et al. 2010], or through an external attacker who takes physical possession of the system (like a laptop or desktop) [Tereshkin 2010]. Collectively, hardware threats can be grouped into three categories. The first category is the side channel attack [Karri et al. 2001, Standaert et al. 2009, Wang et al. 2009, Tiri 2007]. This type of attack compromises the system by capturing information about program execution, such as electromagnetic signals emitted due to computations [Fiori and Musolino 2001, Gandolfi et al. 2001], or by exploiting weaknesses in caches and branch predictors [Aciiçmez 2007, Kong et al. 2008, Aciiçmez et al. 2010]. The second category requires physical access to the system. By gaining access to the system, the attacker can launch attacks against encrypted disks, or make the system boot from a compromised OS, or compromise an external device such as the Ethernet card.[5] Finally, the third category of hardware threats consists of hardware Trojans. A hardware Trojan is a malicious circuitry, or malicious modification of circuitry, inserted into the computer system [Jin et al. 2009, Tehranipoor and Koushanfar 2010, Clark et al. 2009, Wang et al. 2008, Potkonjak et al. 2009]. This circuit can be inserted during any phase of the chip design and fabrication: specification phase, design phase, validation phase, physical design phase, fabrication phase, or deployment. The Trojan is typically dormant and is triggered only after some event, such as the execution of a specific instruction sequence, or external signals, etc. When triggered, the Trojan can disable some hardware fences, cause denial of service, leak information, or cause the system to malfunction. How do we defend against all that?

Integrity checking to detect control flow anomalies at runtime involves computing a hash value of an instruction or a basic block at compile time and comparing it with the hash value calculated at runtime [Schuette and Shen 1987, Gelbart et al. 2005, Gassend et al. 2003]. At a microarchitecture level, the instruction can be modified to secure the system against malicious code injection [Fiskiran and Lee 2004]. This technique of course has some performance effect because it controls the processor pipeline and does not commit the instructions in the basic block until integrity has been checked.

For multicore processors, Orthrus [Huang et al. 2010] employs replication of the program on multiple cores to enhance security. At runtime, these replicas execute on different cores with the same input, and their outputs are checked for

---

5. http://www.theregister.co.uk/2010/11/23/network card rootkit/.

consistency. Since it is much more difficult for an adversary to successfully compromise all the replicas without causing detectable divergence, the system is more secure at the expense of efficient hardware usage. SHIELD [Patel and Parameswaran 2008] uses a dedicated security processor that monitors the applications running on the other processors.

There are still several open questions:

- We need to ensure that the schemes used to ensure security are scalable to large numbers of nodes.

- We need to carefully model the effect on power and performance.

- We need to extend the system to different types of accelerators.

Ensuring the security of systems is one of many factors affecting performance. Bandwidth is another important factor.

3.5 Bandwidth

We are facing a bandwidth wall both off-chip and at higher levels (among blades, cabinets, etc.). With a large number of cores per chip and a huge number of processors and computing nodes in high-performance computing machines, we expect potential performance gains but also severe performance bottlenecks: the expected increase of bandwidth requirements.

Software applications are becoming much more sophisticated and are characterized by large memory footprints. This means an increase in the number of cache memory misses and more accesses to off-chip memory, which, in turn, puts a lot of pressure on memory ports, memory buses, and socket pins, and severely affects overall performance. As we go from on-chip to off-chip to on-board to blades and all the way to cabinets, the bandwidth required is higher but the bandwidth given by technology is lower. For instance, on-chip bandwidth is much higher than off-chip. Solving the bandwidth problem needs different solutions at different levels. Dealing with on-chip is different than off-chip, which is different than among computing nodes, and so on, because the bandwidth requirement is different and the technology used is different. Let's see how we can approach the bandwidth wall at one level: managing off-chip bandwidth. We did some experiments and we present here some insights.

3.5.1 Adventures with Off-Chip Bandwidth

A traditional memory system, DRAM, can be optimized for latency or bandwidth but not both. So we have latency-optimized memory for CPUs and bandwidth-optimized memory for GPUs—another manifestation of heterogeneity. Most of the work related to memory systems in academia/industry focuses on managing the interconnection network, reducing power consumption, or designing an efficient memory system (in terms of number of cache misses). However, off-chip bandwidth has always been thought of as a technological, rather than an architectural, problem, unlike on-chip bandwidth requirements. Any cache miss leaves the potential for a lot of traffic, not only for bringing the missed block but also for writing back victimized dirty blocks (i.e., blocks chosen by the cache replacement policy to be evicted from the cache). This bandwidth requirement affects performance, and leads to power dissipation and a consumption increase in interconnects, off-chip interface, memory controllers, and memory banks. Most of the current multicore architectures use a shared on-chip last-level cache (LLC). Since off-chip traffic is mostly generated by this on-chip LLC, this LLC needs to be bandwidth friendly with as little hardware overhead and as little negative impact to performance as possible. Let's assume, for the sake of this adventure but without loss of generality, that we have a multicore processor with a two-level cache hierarchy. The LLC is level two. Let's also assume the LLC is using least-recently-used (LRU) replacement policy. LRU is not really used in real processors, but it is the basic algorithm from which other, more practical, policies have emerged.

We experimented with a SPLASH-2 benchmark suite [Woo et al. 1995] on a multicore chip of four cores.[6] Figure 3.9 shows the percentage of LLC accesses for which the LRU block of the accessed set is found dirty. We can see that, on average, whenever the LLC (in our case, the L2 cache) is accessed, 69.5% of the time the LRU block of the accessed set is dirty. This means a high chance of generating writebacks, which leads to off-chip traffic. We aim at decreasing the amount of traffic going toward the memory without increasing the traffic coming from the memory. That is, we want to decrease the amount of data written back to off-chip memory without increasing cache misses.

The traffic generated by the LLC is the result of the replacement policy used in this cache. There are many excellent replacement policies available in the literature [Jeong and Dubois 2003; Yang et al. 2005; Kharbutli and Solihin 2005; Qureshi et al. 2006, 2007; Sheikh and Kharbutli 2010; Jaleel et al. 2008, 2015]. Their main goal is to reduce read misses, but they do not consider the effect on bandwidth requirement.

The LRU block is victimized. But what happens if we try to victimize a non-LRU block? And why do we victimize non-LRU blocks? There is a common belief that

---

6. We have chosen the benchmarks with the largest memory footprint from the SPLASH-2 suite. The input set of the benchmarks does not vary with the number of cores.

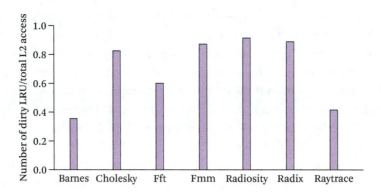

Figure 3.9   Ratio of dirty LRU blocks to the total number of Accesses in the LLC.

non-LRU blocks are important blocks and that getting rid of them hurts performance. This is true for an L1 cache. But is it true for an LLC? Table 3.3 provides evidence that violating the LRU strategy, of victimizing the LRU block, at the LLC does not always lead to severe performance loss. The table shows the total execution time, in terms of number of cycles, of the whole execution of SPLASH-2 benchmarks for several non-LRU schemes normalized to the LRU scheme. LRU-M means we always victimize the Mth block from the LRU stack. For an 8-way set-associative cache, which is the one we use in this experiment, LRU-7 is the most-recently-used (MRU) block. As we see from the table, even when we always victimize the MRU block, the performance loss can be as little as 6%. Of course this is application dependent and hardware dependent. But it is an insight that may help to direct building future systems. This gives us an idea about what to expect if we deviate from traditional LRU. This means that the *LRU stack in the LLC is no longer an LRU stack, and does not represent recency behavior for the running multithreaded application.* There are two reasons for such a surprising behavior. First, the LLC contains blocks that have exhausted their temporal locality at L1 (or upper-level caches in case of more than two levels). Therefore, blocks at the LLC have less temporal locality than L1, which makes the concept of *recency* at the LRU stack of the LLC less meaningful. The second reason is that the LRU stack at the LLC is the result of interference of LRU stacks of L1 caches (each core has its own L1 caches), so if the interference is destructive, it no longer represents recency information for any single thread, nor for the whole program. Different threads have their own *important* blocks, and hence their own LRU stack. When these threads share a cache, the LRU stack of that cache is not really very useful. Thus the LRU stack is a "mix" of LRU stacks of L1 caches, which may not yield a recency order of any running thread. Sometimes

Table 3.3 Normalized values of the number of cycles for victimizing a non-LRU block

Scheme/Bench	Barnes	Cholesky	Fft	Fmm	Radiosity	Radix	Raytrace
LRU	1	1	1	1	1	1	1
LRU-1	1	1.03	1.01	1	1.01	1	1.02
LRU-2	1	1.06	1	1	1.01	1.04	1.06
LRU-3	1	1.15	1.01	1	1.03	1.07	1.12
LRU-4	1.02	1.23	1.01	1.03	1.03	1.09	1.21
LRU-5	1.04	1.37	1.02	1.06	1.03	1.12	1.36
LRU-6	1.13	1.55	1.04	1.12	1.05	1.18	1.63
LRU-7	1.46	1.69	1.06	1.21	1.09	1.25	2.05

this interference is constructive, which happens when there is a high percentage of shared blocks. Programs with such constructive interference are LRU friendly, such as Raytrace, for example, and are negatively affected by victimizing non-LRU blocks.

Further evidence that the strict order of the LRU stack is losing its importance is shown in Figure 3.10. The figure shows the stack hit ratios of the LRU stack for one, four, and eight cores for some of the SPLASH-2 benchmark suite. For one core, the result is expected and known; the majority of the hits occur at the MRU position. But as we increase the number of cores, which in our case increases the number of threads, the MRU block becomes less important. Are these findings of any use to us? Let's see.

We need to try several things. Let's start with a simple static technique. Suppose we have an *n*-way associative cache. The blocks are placed from position 1 to *n* with the most-recently-used block at position 1 and the least at position *n*. In a regular LRU, whenever a new block has to be placed in the cache, the block at position *n* (the LRU block) is evicted. In our experiment, let's call it *modified LRU* (MLRU); we choose to victimize a clean block between LRU and LRU−M. This saves bandwidth by retaining the dirty blocks in the cache as long as possible. If, however, all the blocks from LRU to LRU−M are dirty, the LRU block is chosen to be evicted like in the regular replacement policy. For example, if M = 3, the technique would look for the first nondirty block starting from LRU to LRU−3 and victimize it. There is one parameter for this scheme: M. This parameter designates how many blocks we will examine to determine the victim. M = 1 is the traditional LRU since it means that we will examine only one block, which is the LRU. M = *n* means we will look at

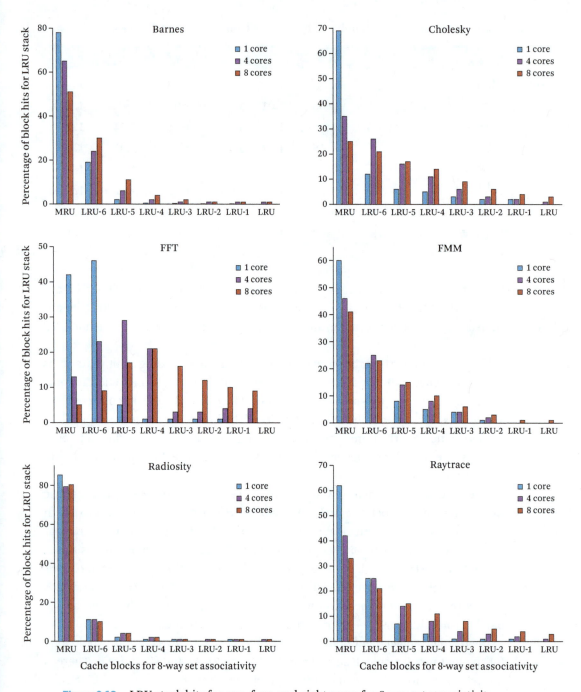

Figure 3.10   LRU stack hits for one, four, and eight cores for 8-way set associativity.

the LRU blocks and $n - 1$ other blocks on top of it in the LRU stack. So for an 8-way set-associative cache, the maximum M is 8. M is determined at design time and is not changed afterward.

The main advantage of that static scheme is its simplicity. Once we decide on the design parameter, M in this case, the implementation is fixed. However, determining this design parameter is usually not easy because it depends on runtime information that is not available at design time, so it relies on designer experience and a lot of simulations. Determining M is very challenging and is application dependent. We need a scheme where M changes dynamically, depending on the application behavior. We can try some schemes for dynamically changing M, such as *writeback-sensitive* and *LRU-sensitive*. Each of these schemes can either be global (same M for the whole cache) or local (M per set). In the writeback-sensitive scheme, when M is high, we have a higher chance of reducing traffic but also a higher chance of affecting performance. This means that M is governed by how much traffic (writebacks) is generated, and this traffic is generated only in the case of a cache miss at the LLC. So in the writeback-sensitive scheme, M is incremented when there is a writeback, to reduce off-chip traffic, and is decremented when there is a cache miss with no writeback, to reduce performance loss. The new value of M will be used the next time a victim is to be chosen. In the LRU-sensitive scheme, we check the LRU block every time the cache is accessed to see whether it is dirty. If it is, then we have potential traffic if we victimize the LRU block, so we increment M to reduce potential traffic. We decrement M whenever there is a cache miss, at the LLC, to reduce potential performance loss. The technique works on the premise that if the LRU is made dirty, then there are more chances of a writeback, so we increase the value of M to check more blocks for a clean one. If, however, the application is LRU friendly, it will result in misses and each miss would reduce the value of M, bringing it back to 1 (LRU). Thus this scheme tries to reduce potential bandwidth. It assumes implicitly that a dirty LRU will generate bandwidth. This assumption is not correct all the time. This is why the former proposed scheme (writeback-sensitive) turns out to be better. We will show results of these experiments shortly. But for now let's continue our brainstorming for reducing off-chip bandwidth by manipulating LLC replacement policy.

In order to reduce the complexity of the hardware, compiler support can be used. Compilers are essentially free in terms of hardware requirements. We will use compiler-based profiling. The compiler will use one core to do only profiling. During profiling the compiler builds a write frequency vector (WFV). WFV is just a histogram representation of the number of writebacks at several time intervals.

During profiling the compiler keeps a count of the number of writebacks at each interval of length X. Then, based on that number, an entry of the WFV is incremented by one. In our experiments we made the compiler check the number of writebacks every 10,000 cycles. We have a WFV of 32 elements, where each element represents an interval of 10. For example, if the number of writebacks in an interval is 75, it will increment the element number 7 in the WFV. The above numbers are empirically based on the SPLASH-2 suite but can be easily changed. After the profiling phase, the compiler has a WFV representing a writeback distribution for the application at hand. The following step removes noise from the WFV. We define *noise* as any entries that are smaller than 5% of the largest value in the WFV, and we remove them. This noise-removal step is necessary because we want our algorithms to be based on frequent behavior, not some individual rare events. With the noise-free WFV, we propose two algorithms: a frequency-based algorithm and a weighted-average algorithm.

For a frequency-based algorithm, given a noise-free WFV:

- Pick the two indices for the highest and lowest numbers above the noise level
- Min = highest number of the interval represented by the lowest index
- Max = lowest number of the interval represented by the highest index

For example, if the two indices were 7 for the lowest and 20 for the highest, Min would be 69 and Max would be 199. Min and Max represent two thresholds that will be used at runtime. These two thresholds are given to the hardware. Every X cycles, the hardware keeps a count of the number of writebacks from the LLC in that interval. This count will either fall below Min, between Min and Max, or above Max. If it is below Min, the LLC uses traditional LRU for victim selection because it means that we have low numbers of replacements of dirty blocks and we do not want to risk losing performance. If the number of writebacks is between Min and Max, we use MLRU with M = associativity/2, as indicated in the previous section. Finally, a number above Max means we have a lot of writebacks, so we use MLRU with M = associativity.

For the weighted-average algorithm, Min and Max are used as they are in the frequency-based algorithm, but Min is always 0 and Max is calculated as $\sum_{i=0}^{32} \frac{WFV_i * mid_i}{SUM}$, where WFV_i is the content of element i of the WFV vector, mid_i is the midrange of element i (for example, if we are talking about element 6, it spans range 50 to 59 with mid of 55), and SUM is the sum of all nonnoisy entries of all WFVs. So in this algorithm we have only two regions: below Max (where we use MLRU with M = associativity/2) and above Max (where we use MLRU with

M = associativity). Max can be thought of as the weighted average of the indices based on their entries. The hardware execution is similar to the frequency-based algorithm above.

One last comment on the above thresholds is that they were computed through profiling with a single core but will be used in a multicore environment. With multicore, and hence multithreading, the traffic is expected to be higher due to the increase in misses (coherence miss), coherence traffic, etc. So before using these thresholds, we multiply them by the total number of cores.

We can combine compiler support with dynamic adaptation. The hardware will start with the above thresholds but will adjust them dynamically based on the behavior. It will keep track of the number of writes every X cycles, as indicated above. The main difference is when an *event* occurs. An event is defined as a situation where half or all the sets in the cache have dirty LRUs. Whenever this event occurs, the counter that keeps track of dirty LRUs is reset if all the sets have dirty LRUs, and Max is updated as follows. If the number of writes (numWRITES) at the current time frame (which is every X cycles) is larger than the current Max, then the *newMax = numWRITES − delta*/4, where delta is the difference of numWRITES and currentMax. Min is adjusted in a way to make the difference between Min and Max constant. The 4 does not represent the number of cores, but it means adding to numWRITES 25% of the difference, which decreases the effect of some bursty noisy behavior. For the weighted-average method, there is no Min.

After all these suggested techniques to reduce off-chip bandwidth traffic in a multicore processor, what are the results we obtained?

We compare each technique by looking at the following parameters:

Number of writebacks.   This is the traffic from the LLC to the memory, and it is our measure of success.

Number of read misses.   This is the traffic from the memory to the LLC. A write miss is considered a read miss followed by a write hit.

Number of cycles.   Of interest here are the total number of cycles taken by the program till completion. So we are trying to reduce the number of writebacks (our main measure of success) while not increasing the number of read misses (negative side effect), and with minimal impact to the total number of cycles.

Our first set of experiments compares traditional LRU with MLRU for different values of M. Figure 3.11 shows the number of writebacks normalized to LRU. All the benchmarks show a decrease in the number of writebacks. The maximum

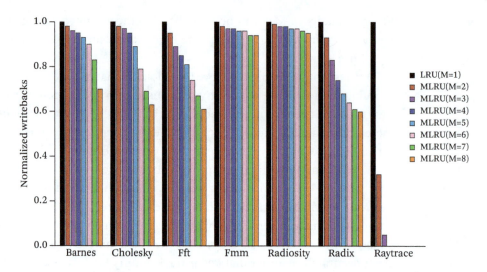

Figure 3.11   Normalized number of writebacks for MLRU.

reduction in writebacks is shown by `Raytrace` in which the writebacks are reduced to near 0. This means that most of the writebacks for that application were for local variables that are no longer needed or for register spills. That is, they are dead values. `Raytrace` and `Cholesky` show a decrease of 36.8% and 93.9%, respectively.

Although we have reduced the traffic going from the LLC to off-chip, we want to be sure that we have not increased the traffic coming from off-chip to memory. Figure 3.12 shows the normalized number of read misses for different values of M. For most benchmarks the increase in misses is less than 15% except for `Barnes`, which has an increase in misses of 56.9%. The high increase in misses of `Barnes` means that it is LRU friendly and it has high temporal locality. For FFT and `Cholesky` we even see a decrease in the number of misses by 16% and 14%, respectively. This means that LRU is not always the best replacement policy, and it is better sometimes to *violate* LRU to gain reduction in off-chip bandwidth.

Figure 3.13 shows the total number of cycles normalized to the LRU scheme. For three benchmarks (FFT, `Cholesky`, and `Radix`), we see an increase in performance since the number of cycles has decreased. This is because we decreased delay caused by bus contention and memory port contention in addition to a reduced miss penalty because the victim is overwritten, not written back. For the benchmarks that have an increase in misses, we expect some performance loss. Only three benchmarks show a decrease in performance, out of which two benchmarks have an increase in the number of cycles less than 1%, except for `Barnes`,

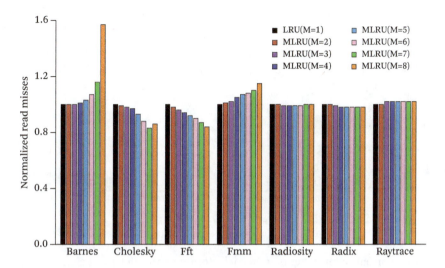

Figure 3.12 Normalized number of read misses for MLRU.

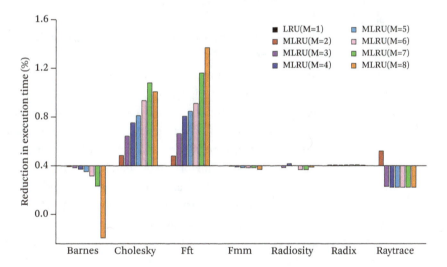

Figure 3.13 Speedup.

which is 7.5%. By using $M = 3$ or $M = 4$, we guarantee good performance. For the rest of the results, we use MLRU with $M = 4$ as our main static technique to compare with other techniques. Also for the rest of the experiments, we drop FMM and `Radix` due to their very low number of writebacks.

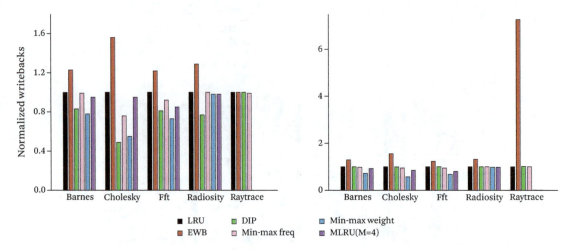

Figure 3.14 Normalized number of writebacks for four cores (left) and eight cores (right) (compiler support and static schemes).

Let's now add compiler support to the static scheme. Figure 3.14 shows the normalized number of writebacks. We compare LRU with eager writeback [Lee et al. 2000](a compromise between write-through and writeback), DIP [Qureshi et al. 2007](dynamic insertion policy), our techniques using compiler support (frequency-based and weighted-average), and MLRU with M = 4. The best three schemes for four cores are the weighted-average, M = 4, and DIP. However, the weighted-average becomes better as we increase the number of cores to eight, which is a sign of good scalability. The frequency-based method does well too, but the LRU part of it (when number of writebacks is below Min) holds it a step behind the weighted-average. Similar behavior can be seen in the number of misses shown in Figure 3.15. As the number of cores increases, the compiler-based weighted-average method and static MLRU with M = 4 do much better. The proposed techniques do not hurt performance, as indicated by Figure 3.16.

Raytrace is the only benchmark that suffers some performance loss. This is because the interference at the LLC among the threads is constructive (blocks shared by more than one core account for 99% of the blocks at the LLC), which makes the program very sensitive to block replacement, as was indicated earlier in Table 3.3.

Let's now see how our dynamic techniques + compiler support behave. We experimented with the four variations of the dynamic techniques: writeback-sensitive and LRU-sensitive, with each one using local or global M. We found that the global scheme is better from a price-performance point of view. The gain we get from the

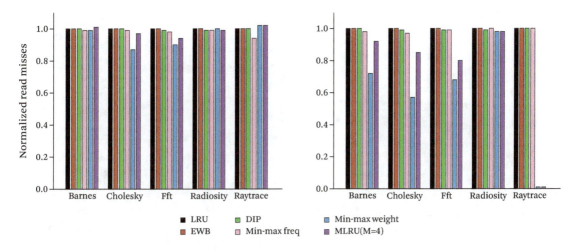

Figure 3.15 Normalized number of read misses for four cores (left) and eight cores (right) (compiler support and static schemes).

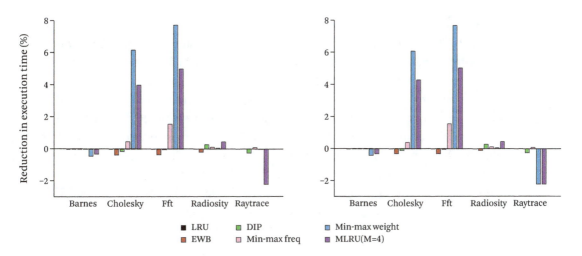

Figure 3.16 Speedup for four cores (left) and eight cores (right) (compiler support and static schemes).

local scheme does not justify the extra hardware. The writeback-sensitive technique is better than LRU-sensitive techniques for most of the benchmarks. So we will be using writeback-sensitive with global M as our dynamic technique (we will call it *dynamic M*). Figure 3.17 compares the total number of writebacks normalized to LRU. The weighted-average and dynamic M schemes are the best on average. This

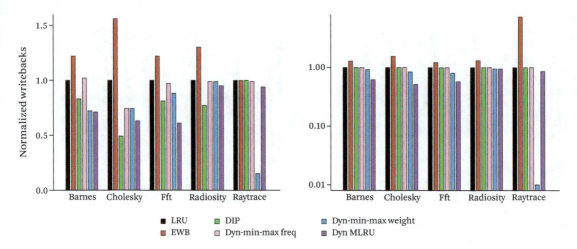

Figure 3.17   Normalized number of writebacks for four cores (left) and eight cores (right) (compiler support and dynamic schemes).

means that they are the most accurate at capturing block behavior. The LRU component of the frequency-based scheme affects its ability to save on off-chip bandwidth.

Figure 3.18 compares the same techniques in terms of read misses. With the exception of Barnes, dynamic M and weighted-average methods are the best on average, together with DIP. To understand the behavior of Barnes, it is important to see the number of dirty blocks it has. Figure 3.19 shows the percentage of dirty blocks to the total number of blocks at the LLC for Barnes over time. There are phases where this program has 80% of its blocks dirty. This causes M to be very high, which increases the likelihood of discarding an important block, because high values of M affect Barnes performance, as indicated by Table 3.3 earlier. This also explains the speedup (and slowdown) shown in Figure 3.20.

What is the moral of the story? We can see from all the above that

- Bandwidth is a performance bottleneck and a big challenge.
- We are using a very diverse set of applications with different requirements, another source of heterogeneity.
- It is very challenging to deal with bandwidth without affecting other factors like performance.
- The problem becomes more challenging as the number of cores and threads increases.

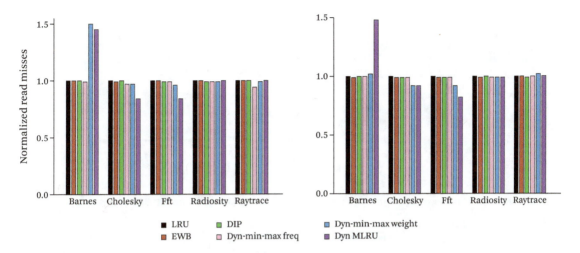

Figure 3.18   Normalized number of read misses for four cores (left) and eight cores (right) (compiler support and dynamic schemes).

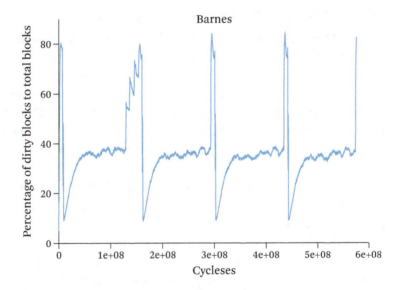

Figure 3.19   Percentage of dirty blocks to total blocks for Barnes.

All of those scenarios were for off-chip bandwidth. Once we are off-chip, we need to deal with bandwidth at higher granularities: among chips on-board, among boards in blades, among blades in cabinets, and among cabinets.

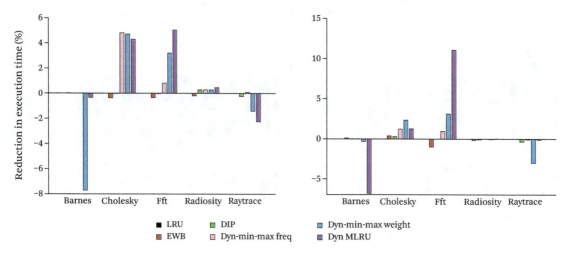

Figure 3.20 Speedup for four cores (left) and eight cores (right) (compiler support and dynamic schemes).

3.5.2 What About Bandwidth Walls at Other Levels?

At a higher level of granularity, dealing with bandwidth depends on several factors. One factor is the implementation, which consists of the technology used (copper vs optical) and the protocol and signaling used, as we discussed earlier in this chapter. Another very important factor is *data locality*. As you may have guessed, this means structuring your parallel program so that processes (or threads) have the data they need near where they execute. This reduces the need for frequent data movement, and this is a big advantage by itself. Energy efficiency of wires is not improving, and computation cost is much lower than communication cost.

Data locality depends mainly on the programmer. The compiler and OS can have a role, but the programmer knows the program well and can structure it accordingly. The main issue here is that this complicates the task of the programmer and affects productivity. Therefore, data locality abstraction is a need. *Data locality abstraction* is a way of expressing computations so that information about proximity of data can be communicated to an optimizing software stack [Unat et al. 2017]. The abstraction takes several forms: libraries, data structures, languages, or runtime. Other tools that can help in data abstraction are debuggers, profilers, and of course compilers. If done well, and it is still an ongoing task, data locality abstraction will boost programmers' productivity and will be a big step toward performance portability.

Compilers currently have some kind of abstraction in parallel languages. Some have local data by default (e.g., MPI), some have global data by default (e.g., PGAS languages), and some do not expose anything to the programmer (e.g., OpenMP). PGAS are easier to adopt but harder to get performance easily.

In order to have runtime support for data locality abstraction, we need to have two models: an application model and an architecture model. The application model consists of a set of metrics that presents the application's behavior, for example, an affinity graph. This is still an active research topic. The architecture model encompasses computation nodes and their heterogeneity, communication cost, and memory access cost. Using these two models, the runtime can optimize data movement with minimum effort on the part of the programmer.

3.6 In Conclusion

In this chapter we went from inside the chip to the system level. We saw how to integrate several chips to make a big machine. The design manifests itself in different forms: the type of computing nodes, the interconnection, and the memory hierarchy. In very large machines, such as supercomputers, the interconnect is usually implemented at several levels: within a chip, within nodes, within blades, within cabinets, and among cabinets. These levels of interconnect introduce a severe level of heterogeneity in data movement latency, not to mention the heterogeneity in number-crunching performance introduced by the different computing nodes. How to program those types of heterogeneous machines? This is the topic of the next chapter.

Programmability

One of the main success factors of a hardware design is its programmability. No matter how fast or power efficient the designed machine is, if it is not easy to program, it has high chances of failure. The Cell processor is a good example of that, even though there are some other factors that contributed to its failure, but programmability is for sure an important factor.

This chapter discusses the issue of programmability. What do programmers want? What do we currently have in terms of programmability of heterogeneous systems? Can we do better?

4.1 Wish List of a Programmer

If you ask programmers from different domains and expertise about what they wish to have from a perfect programming language, most probably each programmer will start thinking a bit, then give you an ad hoc list. If you look at the lists from different programmers, you will find many conflicting requirements. So you come to the conclusion that there is no such thing as a perfect programming language. However, we can find new programming languages created every several months! Which is an indication that there is a lot to be desired from programming languages. But didn't we get enough expertise in the last seven decades to design a *perfect* programming language? The answer brings up more questions: Perfect for what? And executing on what? Over the last several decades the types of machines on which we execute our programs have changed dramatically. So, too, have the types of applications. So a perfect programming language is really a moving target because it depends on the application at hand, the type of machine executing the application, and the mentality of the programmer.

Usually, the need for a new programming model arises at inflection points in computing history: for example, VLIW, the move to multicore, exascale computing, quantum computing, the Internet of Things (IoT), and, of course, the rise of heterogeneous computing.

If we can have a short list for what programmers wish from a perfect programming language (list not exhaustive by any means), we can say the following:

- Programmers need to be productive. This short time-to-market puts a lot of stress on programmers. Stress means more bugs. More bugs mean delay, which increases the stress. So productivity is important. There have been many studies about productivity of programming languages [Cantonnet et al. 2004, Billingsley et al. 2010]. The hard question is how to measure productivity. Researchers have tried different things, like the number of lines of code, number of keywords, number of characters, etc. Each measurement has its own pros and cons.

- Related to the previous point, a language needs to have a good set of libraries built for it so that programmers do not need to reinvent the wheel or do many low-level tweaks. This increases programmers' productivity.

- Professional programmers like to have full control (e.g., assigning threads to cores, reducing or increasing the voltage and frequency). Some languages provide APIs for this lower-level control. But this comes at the expense of productivity.

- Programming languages must ensure portability. This may come at the expense of full control because you may tweak your code and use as much optimization as possible to get the best performance on a specific machine. If you try to execute the code on a machine with different characteristics (e.g., caches with different block sizes or associativity, or different types of interconnection), then you may not get the expected performance or you may even get slowdown. Virtualization comes to the rescue in these circumstances, but at the expense of performance loss due to overhead.

- The programming language must ensure a homogeneous look at the environment. Heterogeneity is hard. If the language hides much of the underlying heterogeneity from you, things will be easier but at the expense of full control.

- Programmers wish that the language and its associated runtime give the highest performance. The runtime of the language must then have low overhead and smart dynamic optimizations.

Suppose we, magically, designed a programming language with the above characteristics. Will this help *all* programmers with their code? The answer depends on psychology.

4.2

Psychology of Programming

The term *psychology of programming* is used to designate the field that studies the psychological aspects of writing programs. We do not want to go deep into psychology here. But in this section we try to extract some aspects that designate expert programmers and use them to come up with a list of programming language characteristics that can help programmers do their job well. Then we use this information to update/refine the list we made in Section 4.1.

In the book *Psychology of Programming* edited by Hoc [1990], there is an interesting chapter titled "Expert Programmers and Programming Languages" by Marian Petre about how expert programmers use programming languages. One of the things mentioned in that chapter is that experts represent programs in terms of semantic structure, unlike novices who think syntactically. I can personally confirm this too, when I teach undergraduate students versus graduate students (or strong undergrad students). Average undergrad students, especially in freshman or sophomore classes, tend to concentrate more on the syntax of the language than the philosophy of the language or the way of thinking using the underlying programming model. The chapter also mentions that experts spend more time planning. Let me stop at this planning thing to discuss an important point: picking the right algorithm, as things have changed a lot lately.

Let's take the big-O notation in algorithm analysis. Our students learn how to analyze algorithms and pick or design algorithms based on the asymptotic behavior of computations of the worst-case scenario, also known as the big-O notation. Is this the best way to analyze algorithms, with the machines we have now? You can optimize your algorithm to have lower complexity, that is, a lower amount of computation. But this may come at the expense of data movement (communication overhead) and memory access. Communication and memory access are way more expensive than computations today. This means you can find that an algorithm of $O(n \log n)$ can be slower than another one of $O(n^2)$. The moral of this example, and also pointed out in the aforementioned book, is that expert programmers think at different levels.

Expert programmers want the ability to think in abstract form, in high-level constructs, and also the ability to manipulate the hardware. That is, as the book mentions, they need to choose their grain of focus at different times. This is how they are productive. A programming language needs to provide that. One of the main reasons programmers may need to have control over low-level details is to be able to predict the behavior and control of their programs. If a programmer thinks only in terms of algorithm and language syntax but knows nothing about the cache hierarchy, cache organization, the interconnect, whether the processor has superscalar capability and out of order execution, whether each core supports multiple threads, etc., then the programmer will be in total darkness when it comes to performance. If power efficiency is added to the list, then the programmer may want control over the frequency and voltage of each core. If reliability comes into question, then more hardware details must be revealed. For instance, shall transient errors be exposed to the programmer? Or dealt with under the hood, especially in supercomputers and large datacenters?

It should be noted that we are talking about expert programmers, designing and writing programs for heterogeneous parallel machines to get the best performance per watt. So applications that don't have this requirement can just use programming languages that protect the programmer from low-level details, for the sake of productivity. In that case productivity means finishing your programming task fast, and not having to worry about performance, power, reliability, etc.

But shall we disregard productivity even for high performance? Definitely not, because there is an economic angle here that involves time-to-market, customer satisfaction, etc. The point is to have a programming language that can give the programmer the ability to think and implement at a high level, as well as the ability to think and act on the low-level details. As languages mature and more versatile application pools arise, programmers build more libraries, and levels of abstraction are built to make things easier from a productivity perspective.

Given all the above, we can now modify the list from Section 4.1 to be as follows. The wish list of programming language characteristics for expert programmers:

- Programmers need to be productive. But productivity here does not only mean finishing your programming task fast. It means finishing it on time and fulfilling the requirements of performance, power, reliability, etc. For this to happen, the programmer needs to be able to access low-level details, when needed, and high-level structures alike. A good programming language must provide both.

- Programming languages must ensure portability. Your program may need to be deployed on machines with different characteristics in terms of number and type of computing elements, memory hierarchy, and so on. There are several strategies to deal with this. The first is for the language to provide high-level constructs and let the runtime deal with the low-level details. Many #pragma-based languages (OpenMP, OpenACC, etc.) took this route. However, this comes at the expense of some control revoked from the programmer, at different degrees depending on the language. The second route is to bare it all to the programmer to write extra code to detect the underlying system settings and, based on that, use different functions/libraries/algorithms. The third strategy is to modify the code on the fly, using techniques like continuous compilation [Childers et al. 2003] or binary optimization [Hazelwood 2011]. The holy grail of high-performance computing, though, is performance portability. Of course if your program runs on a weaker machine, you will see performance degradation. But if it runs on a comparable machine but with different settings (different interconnect, for example), you must see close performance.

- The programming language must ensure a homogeneous look at the environment. If we relate this to the first point on our list, then the correct thing is for the language to give a homogeneous look at the environment but give more details, that is, heterogeneity is revealed, if the programmer needs to make low-level modifications.

- Runtime of the system must have low overhead. This item is unchanged from our previous list.

Now that we are done with our wish list, let's come back to real life. Are we even close to having such a language? What do we have now?

4.3 What Do We Have? The Current Status Quo

There are several parallel programming models around. For each model there are several implementations (i.e., several programming languages). The implementation can be either a totally new language or additions to languages through pragmas or libraries. In this section we take a quick tour of some parallel programming paradigms that target heterogeneous systems.

To make the comparison easier, we will use a simple example that is embarrassingly parallel as our running example, a simple vector addition. The sequential version of it is shown in Listing 4.1. To concentrate on the parallelism part, we neglect any error checking/handling in the code shown in this chapter. The two functions get_the_data() and process_array() populate the two arrays A and B with data and process the resulting array C. Their source code is not shown here as it is not important to our discussion. You may wonder why vector addition is suitable for heterogeneous systems and not traditional homogeneous systems. If the number of elements in the two vectors to be added is small (e.g., a few thousand), then a few homogeneous cores are enough. Once the two vectors become huge (e.g., millions or billions), then we need accelerators like GPUs or many-core chips like Xeon Phi, for example, to finish the computations fast. If the data in these vectors

Listing 4.1 Serial version of vector addition

```
1  #include <stdio.h>
2
3  #define N 1000000
4
5  int main()
6  {
7    int * A;
8    int * B;
9    int * C;
10
11   int i;
12
13   A = (int *)malloc(N*sieof(int));
14   B = (int *)malloc(N*sieof(int));
15   C = (int *)malloc(N*sieof(int));
16
17   get_the_data(A, B);  //Fill the two arrays
18
19   for( i = 0; i < N; i++)
20     C[i] = A[i] + B[i];
21
22   process_array(C);
23
24   free(A);
25   free(B);
26   free(C);
27
28   return 0;
29 }
```

are generated in real time (i.e., streamed) and we need to process them on the spot, then something like FPGAs are suitable for the job. Now, let's dive into our chosen paradigms.

4.3.1 MPI

MPI[1] is a de facto programming model for distributed memory architectures, challenged only with PGAS (partitioned global address space) models. MPI is just a library and set of APIs used on top of common languages like C/C++ and Fortran.

_____

1. https://www.open-mpi.org/

You don't want to use Java or Python on a distributed memory system, do you? We are talking about performance here! With MPI several processes are created, using the command line by the user. Since we are talking about processes, then it means each process has its own address space. Nevertheless, these processes need to exchange data as they are solving the same problem. Data values are exchanged using messages, hence the name MPI (message passing interface). Listing 4.2 shows the MPI version of vector addition. It seems longer, much longer, than the sequential version! As we will shortly see, it is just for setting the stage.

All the created processes execute the same code. In order to avoid redundant computations, we must ensure that each process works on different parts of the problem or does different tasks. To do that, MPI groups processes into something called a *communicator*. By default, all created processes are inside one default communicator called MPI_COMM_World. You can create different groups from this communicator and/or split the communicator if you want. Inside each communicator in our example, we just keep the default communicator. Each process has a unique ID, called a *rank*. Line 14 in the listing just initializes the MPI runtime system and passes to it the arguments of the main() function, if any. Lines 15 and 16 let each process get its rank and the size of the default communicator. That is, after executing lines 15 and 16, each process will know its rank, stored in a variable with the same name, and the variable *size* will have the total number of processes created. Line 48 closes the MPI runtime. You cannot use any API from MPI after line 48. Your program may continue execution as a single process executing C (or C++ or Fortran). By using the rank in an if-condition, you can make each process do different things from each other. Here, the master process, the one with rank 0, dynamically allocates three arrays: A, B, and C. It also populates arrays A and B with data. This is done only by process 0 because of the if-condition in line 22. All the processes, including the master process, dynamically allocate three other arrays, of smaller sizes, called local_a, local_b, and local_c. This is shown in lines 23, 24, and 25.

Because sending messages is very expensive and MPI is usually used in big machines with distributed and large numbers of computing nodes, we use it when the problem size is really huge. Otherwise, we will lose the performance we gained from parallelism due to the overhead of communication. We are using small array sizes in the example of Listing 4.2 just for simplicity. But in real situations, if N is just one million, as in our example here, then MPI is a bad choice. MPI allows two processes to communicate through MPI_Send() and MPI_Receive(). Each send must have a corresponding receive or else you may reach a deadlock because those APIs are usually blocking. That is, MPI_Receive(), when called by a process, blocks

Listing 4.2 MPI version of vector addition

```c
1   #include <stdio.h>
2   #include <mpi.h>
3
4   #define N 1000000
5
6   int main()
7   {
8     int * A, * B, * C;
9     int * local_A, * local_B, * local_C;
10    int i;
11    int size; // the communicator
12    int rank; // the process
13
14    MPI_Init(NULL, NULL);
15    MPI_Comm_size(MPI_COMM_WORLD, &size);
16    MPI_Comm_rank(MPI_COMM_WORLD, &rank);
17
18    local_A = (int *)malloc(ceil(N/size)*sizeof(int));
19    local_B = (int *)malloc(ceil(N/size)*sizeof(int));
20    local_C = (int *)malloc(ceil(N/size)*sizeof(int));
21
22    if(rank == 0){
23      A = (int *)malloc(N*sizeof(int));
24      B = (int *)malloc(N*sizeof(int));
25      C = (int *)malloc(N*sizeof(int));
26      get_the_data(A, B);  //Fill the two arrays
27      MPI_Scatter(A, N/size, MPI_INT,
28          local_A, N/size, MPI_INT, 0, MPI_COMM_WORLD);
29      MPI_Scatter(B, N/size, MPI_INT,
30          local_B, N/size, MPI_INT, 0, MPI_COMM_WORLD);
31    }
32
33    for( i = 0 ; i < N/size; i++)
34      local_C[i] = local_A[i] + local_B[i];
35
36    MPI_Gather(local_C, N/size, MPI_INT,
37        C, N/size, MPI_INT, 0, MPI_COMM_WORLD);
38
39    if(rank == 0) {
40      process_array(C);
41      free(A);
42      free(B);
43      free(C);
44    }
45
46    free(local_A); free(local_B); free(local_C);
47
48    MPI_Finalize();
49
50    return 0;
51  }
```

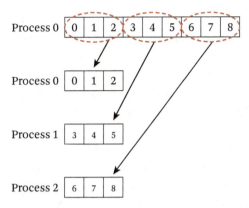

Figure 4.1   A Scatter operation in MPI.

this process till it receives the data from the corresponding MPI_Send(). But in our example here we don't want this one-to-one communication. We need collective communication among processes because it is cheaper than sending one-to-one messages. So the master process takes arrays A and B, cuts them into pieces of equal sizes, and *scatters* them to the other arrays including itself. This is what happens in lines 27–30. Figure 4.1 shows how the scatter is performed. Let's look at one scatter operation and explain it. MPI_Scatter(A, N/size, MPI_INT, local_A, N/size, MPI_INT, 0, MPI_COMM_WORLD) means take the array A from process 0, divide it into chunks of N/size elements, and give those chunks to processes based on their ranks. That is, process 0 takes the first N/size, process 1 takes the next chunk, etc. The receiving processes, including the master process, store those chunks into another array local_A. This API is collective, which means *all* processes must call it or else the program will hang with a deadlock. Each process will do the additions of its chunk (lines 33 and 34). We have parallelism here because all the chunks are added in parallel by the different processes. The following step is to *gather* all these chunks and put them back into the original array C at the address space of process with rank 0 (line 36). Remember that arrays A, B, and C exist only in the address space process 0 (look at lines 23–25). Therefore, only process 0 must free those arrays (lines 39–44). But the local arrays local_a, local_b, and local_c have been allocated by all processes, and hence must be freed by all of them (line 46).

MPI can be used with shared memory models like OpenMP or with accelerator languages like CUDA. A process can offload part of its code to a GPU, for example. MPI also allows you to map processes to cores (affinity). It is an easy-to-grasp language. You can have a parallel program ready to execute from a sequential one with just a few extra lines, but you have to manage communication by hand.

4.3.2 OpenMP

Whereas MPI deals with distributed memory, OpenMP[2](Open Multiprocessing) is gaining popularity in shared memory architectures. Here we are talking about one process executed in parallel using threads sharing the whole address space. These threads share the heap, text, and data, but each thread has its own stack. It is also a library on top of many common languages and is based on pragmas. A quick look at Listing 4.3 reveals that it does not require a lot of stage setting like MPI. Actually, the main difference between the sequential version and the OpenMP version is line 20! This line, simply speaking, tells the OpenMP runtime to generate M threads. The number of iterations of the for-loops (OpenMP works only with for-loops, not while nor do-while) are divided among those M threads. There are several remarks here.

- The number of M threads can be determined by the programmers or the runtime.

- OpenMP does not check for dependencies among iterations. It is the job of the programmer to manage the dependencies and any critical sections that may exist.

- If the work in each loop iteration depends on the loop index, then dividing the iterations evenly among threads may lead to a load imbalance problem. OpenMP gives the programmer the ability to assign loops dynamically (called *schedule*) to threads, depending on some criteria (such as when a thread finishes *x* iterations, it can take more).

- Even though OpenMP was created to parallelize loops, it can also assign different tasks to threads in parallel (called *tasks* and *sections* in OpenMP parlance).

- OpenMP gives the programmer the ability to make some variables shared among all threads and make others private, overriding the default.

The program in Listing 4.3 starts with one process and one thread of execution. That thread executes everything till line 19. The pragma at line 20 forks M processes. Each process will execute a subset of the loop iterations, as we said before. Since in this code the programmer did not indicate the number of threads, then it is up to the runtime to determine it. In most OpenMP implementations, the default number of threads will be the number of cores. The pragma applies only to the

---

2. https://www.openmp.org/

Listing 4.3 OpenMP version of vector addition

```
1   #include <stdio.h>
2   #include <omp.h>
3
4   #define N 1000000
5
6   int main()
7   {
8     int * A;
9     int * B;
10    int * C;
11
12    int i;
13
14    A = (int *)malloc(N*sizeof(int));
15    B = (int *)malloc(N*sizeof(int));
16    C = (int *)malloc(N*sizeof(int));
17
18    get_the_data(A, B);   //Fill the two arrays
19
20    #pragma omp parallel for
21    for( i = 0 ; i < N; i++)
22      C[i] = A[i] + B[i];
23
24    process_array(C);
25
26    free(A);
27    free(B);
28    free(C);
29
30    return 0;
31  }
```

following structured piece of code. In our case here, it is the for-loop. Starting from line 24, we are back to one thread of execution.

Starting with version 4.0, OpenMP can now offload tasks to accelerators like GPUs and FPGAs [der Pas et al. 2017]. This is done with a modifier, called `target`, added to the #pragma. Due to its simplicity and its support for accelerators, hence heterogeneous architecture, OpenMP has gained wider popularity recently. It can be used in tandem with MPI if we have multisocket boards (i.e., nodes), or even a single-socket board with a multicore processor connected together. The processors

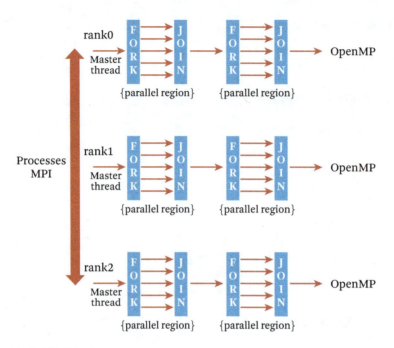

Figure 4.2   Hybrid MPI + OpenMP.

on the board are sharing memory, thus OpenMP. Across boards is distributed memory, thus MPI. This hybrid combination is shown in Figure 4.2. In MPI you explicitly manage communication. In OpenMP communication is implicit, which is easier from a programming perspective but harder to debug and profile.

OpenMP enjoys a very active community and is gaining more and more popularity. Recently, OpenMP started supporting accelerators too.

4.3.3 OpenCL

Open Computing Language (OpenCL)[3] was developed by a consortium of many companies, initiated by Apple and maintained by the Khronos Group [Kaeli et al. 2015]. OpenCL is designed with several goals in mind.

- Maximize portability by minimizing burden on vendors. Take a look at the list of companies in the OpenCL consortium!

- Use all computation resources. (So it is designed with heterogeneous computing in mind.)

---

3. https://www.khronos.org/opencl/

- Drive future hardware requirements.

- Abstract underlying parallelism.

The first requirement makes the host code very tedious, as you can see from Listing 4.4. In order to minimize the burden on vendors, you have to move that burden to the programmer and/or the runtime. Setting the stage here is sophisticated. The second requirement is more or less fulfilled and growing. The third requirement, to the best of my knowledge, is not fulfilled yet, at least not at full scale. The fourth requirement is materialized at the expense of control to the programmer. OpenCL is C-based with a rich library of APIs. It is also a data-parallel language, Single Program Multiple Data (SPMD).

The programming model consists of one host and one or more compute devices. Each compute device consists of one or more compute units. Each compute unit consists of one or more processing elements, as shown in Figure 4.3. This description can be mapped to a wide range of accelerators. As you can see, we did not mention the name of any accelerator (GPU, CPU, etc.), which is the philosophy of OpenCL. See the fourth requirement above.

The host program has some parts that are executed in parallel by the other computation devices. Those parts are called *kernels*. All processing elements execute the same kernel with different data, hence SPMD. Work items are grouped into work groups. So we can say that the OpenCL kernel is the basic unit of parallel code that can be executed on a target compute device. You decide how many work groups and how many work items per work group. Even though all work items in all work groups are executing the same kernel, work items in the same group can synchronize together. It is much cheaper to organize it like this because to be able to synchronize a huge number of work items would be prohibitively expensive in hardware implementation. This is why we see in GPUs, for example, execution units (streaming processors (SPs) or CUDA cores), that are grouped together as streaming multiprocessors (SMs). Threads executed by SPs within the same SM can synchronize together and exchange data faster.

Because OpenCL is designed by a consortium of many companies, there are many implementations of it. Each implementation is called a *platform* (line 35 in Listing 4.4). All platforms follow the standard of OpenCL, of course. But, as with any programming language standard, there are open issues. We saw in OpenMP, for example, that not specifying the number of threads in a parallel section leaves it to the runtime. What the runtime does is implementation dependent. Here also, there are open issues and they are implementation dependent. That is, they are platform dependent.

Listing 4.4 OpenCL version of vector addition

```
1   #include <stdio.h>
2   #include <stdlib.h>
3   #include <CL/cl.h>
4
5   #define N 1000000
6   #define SOURCE_SIZE   100000000
7
8   int main()
9   {
10    int * A, * B, * C;
11    int i;
12
13     A = (int *)malloc(N*sizeof(int));
14     B = (int *)malloc(N*sizeof(int));
15     C = (int *)malloc(N*sizeof(int));
16
17     get_the_data(A, B);  //Fill the two arrays
18
19     // Load the kernel source code into the array source_str
20     FILE *fp;
21     char *source_str;
22     size_t source_size;
23
24     //Read source code
25     fp = fopen("add.cl", "r");
26     source_str = (char*)malloc(MAX_SOURCE_SIZE);
27     source_size = fread( source_str, 1, SOURCE_SIZE, fp);
28     fclose( fp );
29
30     // Get platform and device information
31     cl_platform_id platform_id = NULL;
32     cl_device_id device_id = NULL;
33     cl_uint ret_num_devices;
34     cl_uint ret_num_platforms;
35     cl_int ret = clGetPlatformIDs(1, &platform_id, &ret_num_platforms);
36     ret = clGetDeviceIDs( platform_id, CL_DEVICE_TYPE_DEFAULT, 1,
37             &device_id, &ret_num_devices);
38
39     // Create an OpenCL context
40     cl_context context = clCreateContext( NULL, 1, &device_id, NULL, NULL, &ret);
41
42     // Create a command queue
43     cl_command_queue command_queue = clCreateCommandQueue(context, device_id, 0, &ret);
44
45     // Create memory buffers on the device for each vector
46     cl_mem a_mem = clCreateBuffer(context, CL_MEM_READ_ONLY,
47             N * sizeof(int), NULL, &ret);
48     cl_mem b_mem = clCreateBuffer(context, CL_MEM_READ_ONLY,
49             N * sizeof(int), NULL, &ret);
50     cl_mem c_mem = clCreateBuffer(context, CL_MEM_WRITE_ONLY,
51             N * sizeof(int), NULL, &ret);
```

Listing 4.4   *(continued)*

```
53      // Copy the lists A and B to their respective memory buffers
54      ret = clEnqueueWriteBuffer(command_queue, a_mem_obj, CL_TRUE, 0,
55              N * sizeof(int), A, 0, NULL, NULL);
56      ret = clEnqueueWriteBuffer(command_queue, b_mem_obj, CL_TRUE, 0,
57              N * sizeof(int), B, 0, NULL, NULL);
58
59      // Create a program from the kernel source
60      cl_program program = clCreateProgramWithSource(context, 1,
61              (const char **)&source_str, (const size_t *)&source_size, &ret);
62
63      // Build the program
64      ret = clBuildProgram(program, 1, &device_id, NULL, NULL, NULL);
65
66      // Create the OpenCL kernel
67      cl_kernel kernel = clCreateKernel(program, "vector_add", &ret);
68
69      // Set the arguments of the kernel
70      ret = clSetKernelArg(kernel, 0, sizeof(cl_mem), (void *)&a_mem);
71      ret = clSetKernelArg(kernel, 1, sizeof(cl_mem), (void *)&b_mem);
72      ret = clSetKernelArg(kernel, 2, sizeof(cl_mem), (void *)&c_mem);
73
74      // Execute the OpenCL kernel on the list
75      size_t global_item_size = N; // Process the entire list
76      size_t local_item_size = 100; //Divide work items into groups of 100
77      ret = clEnqueueNDRangeKernel(command_queue, kernel, 1, NULL,
78              &global_item_size, &local_item_size, 0, NULL, NULL);
79
80      // Read the memory buffer C on the device to the local variable C
81      int *C = (int*)malloc(sizeof(int)*N);
82      ret = clEnqueueReadBuffer(command_queue, c_mem, CL_TRUE, 0,
83              N * sizeof(int), C, 0, NULL, NULL);
84
85       process_array(C);
86
87      // Clean up
88      ret = clFlush(command_queue);
89      ret = clFinish(command_queue);
90      ret = clReleaseKernel(kernel);
91      ret = clReleaseProgram(program);
92      ret = clReleaseMemObject(a_mem);
93      ret = clReleaseMemObject(b_mem);
94      ret = clReleaseMemObject(c_mem);
95      ret = clReleaseCommandQueue(command_queue);
96      ret = clReleaseContext(context);
97
98    free(A); free(B); free(C);
99
100   return 0;
101 }
```

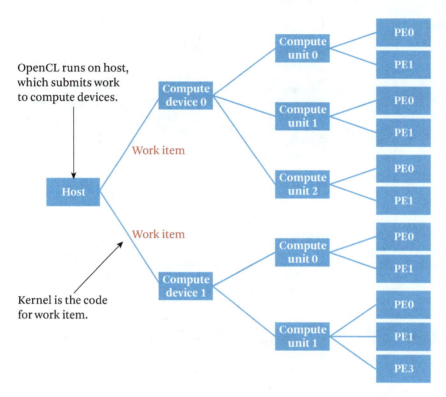

OpenCL runs on host, which submits work to compute devices.

Work item

Host

Work item

Kernel is the code for work item.

Figure 4.3 The OpenCL view of parallelism.

Once you pick a platform, in case your system has several, you need to see which devices are attached (line 36). OpenCL recognizes CPUs, GPUs, FPGAs, and generic accelerators. The next step is to set the stage for executing a program on that platform. Setting the stage for a program is called setting the *context* (line 40). Then you create a command queue from the host to each device (line 43). A command queue is a channel of communication by which the host can send commands to a device. This command can be data transfer, kernel execution, etc. Even though it is called a queue, you can set it up such that commands can be executed out of order, in order, or something in between by setting up dependencies.

Because OpenCL wants to have higher portability with less burden to vendors, it has its own generic memory objects: buffers and images. In the example of Listing 4.4, we use only buffers (lines 46–51); then we include commands in the command queues to move the arrays A and B into these buffers (lines 54–57).

Then comes the most tedious part, which is the designation of the kernel and executing it on the computation device. The kernel can be loaded from a separate

Listing 4.5 OpenCL kernel version of vector addition

```
1  __kernel void vector_add(
2                          __global int *A,
3                          __global int *B,
4                          __global int *C) {
5
6    // Get the index of the current element
7    int i = get_global_id(0);
8
9    C[i] = A[i] + B[i];
10 }
```

source code file (lines 24–28 load the source code of Listing 4.5 into a string). The next step is to create a program (line 60) and build the program (line 64). If the program in the source code has several kernels (in our example here it has only one kernel), then you need to do the create kernel step (line 67) for each. This compiles the kernel for the computation device used. Lines 70–72 specify the arguments for that kernel. You need an API call for each argument. Finally, we are ready to execute the kernel. To specify work groups and work items, we use what is called NDRange (lines 75–78). At the end, you bring the data back to the host (lines 82–83) and clean up (lines 88–98). For the sake of portability and usage with wider computing devices, OpenCL had to sacrifice some programmer productivity and some programmer control. If you have an Intel processor with multicore and embedded GPU as well as a discrete NVIDIA GPU, then OpenCL can be used to execute on all of them in parallel.

4.3.4 OpenACC

OpenACC,[4] or open accelerators, is designed, like OpenMP, to make using accelerators easy for most programmers [Chandrasekaran and Juckeland 2018]. It follows the same philosophy as OpenMP. This group of libraries is relatively new, announced at the annual international supercomputing conference held in 2011. A quick look at Listing 4.6 clearly shows that ease of programming is one of the goals. Programmers can write a sequential version and then annotate it with OpenCL #pragmas. Alas, ease of programming always comes at the expense of more control revoked from the programmer. The loop is parallelized in a way similar to OpenMP and in a philosophy similar to OpenCL. The loop iterations are

---

4. https://www.openacc.org/

Listing 4.6 OpenACC version of vector addition

```c
1  #include <stdio.h>
2
3  #define N 1000000
4
5  int main()
6  {
7     int * A;
8     int * B;
9     int * C;
10    int i;
11
12    A = (int *)malloc(N*sizeof(int));
13    B = (int *)malloc(N*sizeof(int));
14    C = (int *)malloc(N*sizeof(int));
15
16    get_the_data(A, B);  //Fill the two arrays
17
18    #pragma acc parallel loop \
19     copyin(A[0:N-1]) copyin(B[0:N-1]) copyout(C[0:N-1])
20
21    for( i = 0 ; i < N; i++)
22      C[i] = A[i] + B[i];
23
24    process_array(C);
25
26    free(A);
27    free(B);
28    free(C);
29
30    return 0;
31 }
```

distributed among *workers* grouped into *gangs*. You specify the number of gangs and number of workers or you leave it to the runtime, as we did in this example. OpenACC allows for a third level of parallelism (besides gangs and workers) called *vectors*.

4.3.5 CUDA

With GPUs becoming widely used in many applications that are nongraphic, GPU-related languages are becoming widely adopted. Compute unified device architecture (CUDA)[5] is by far one of the most mature and widely adopted languages for using GPUs, especially those from NVIDIA. It was born in 2006, developed and maintained by NVIDIA. Following the same philosophy as OpenCL, a kernel is offloaded from the host to the device (i.e., the GPU). That kernel is executed by a grid that is composed of a group of blocks. Each block is composed of a group of threads. Each thread executes the same kernel but with different data, so we are again using SPMD. As an example, launching a kernel (line 35 of Listing 4.7) has two numbers between triple angle brackets. The first number is the number of blocks and the second number is the number of threads per block. All the blocks form one grid, in CUDA parlance. So we can say that a grid is a kernel in execution (one grid per kernel). Blocks and grids can be designed to be 1D, 2D, or 3D. GPUs and CPUs have their different memory, even if the programming model of the recent versions of CUDA gives the illusion of unified memory. Moving the data between the GPU and CPU is very expensive, so it must be managed carefully either by the programmer or under the hood by the runtime in recent GPU architectures (namely, Pascal and Volta). As we can see from the code, cudaMalloc dynamically allocates space in the device's memory (i.e., the GPU), while malloc dynamically allocates space in the system memory. CUDA can be combined with, for example, OpenMP and MPI.

4.3.6 Heterogeneous System Architecture (HSA)

HSA[6] is not a language per se but a set of specifications that allows seamless movement and execution of data among CPUs and accelerators, like GPUs or FPGAs. It is a cross-vendor initiative, so portability is a goal. The formal definition from Hwu [2015] is "a new hardware platform and associated software stack that allows different types of processors to work together efficiently and cooperatively through shared memory." So it is shared memory. It borrows the setup of queues of commands that we saw in OpenCL and that also exists in CUDA but in a different way (called streams in CUDA). HSA was designed with GPUs in mind. But as computer systems have become more and more heterogeneous, HSA has expanded to include other devices. The code is compiled to an intermediate presentation called heterogeneous system architecture intermediate language (HSAIL). HSAIL is vendor independent. Before execution HSAIL is translated to the ISA of the computing device.

---

5. https://developer.nvidia.com/cuda-zone

6. http://www.hsafoundation.com/

Listing 4.7   CUDA version of vector addition

```
1   #include <stdio.h>
2   #include <cuda.h>
3
4   #define N 1000000
5
6   int main()
7   {
8     int * A;
9     int * B;
10    int * C;
11
12    int * dA;
13    int * dB;
14    int * dC;
15
16
17    int i;
18
19    A = (int *)malloc(N*sizeof(int));
20    B = (int *)malloc(N*sizeof(int));
21    C = (int *)malloc(N*sizeof(int));
22
23
24    cudaMalloc((void **)&dA, N*sizeof(int));
25    cudaMalloc((void **)&dB, N*sizeof(int));
26    cudaMalloc((void **)&dC, N*sizeof(int));
27
28    get_the_data(A, B);  //Fill the two arrays
29
30    // Move the two arrays to the device
31    cudaMemCpy(dA, A, N*sizeof(int), cudaMemcpyHostToDevice);
32    cudaMemcpy(dB, B, N*sizeof(int), cudaMemcpyHostToDevice);
33
34    //Launch the kernel in the device
35    vec_add<<<ceil(N/1024),1024>>>(dA, dB, dC, N);
36
37    //Bring the result back from the device
38    cudaMemCpy(C, dC, N*sizeof(int), cudaMemcpyDeviceToHost);
39
40    process_array(C);
```

Listing 4.7   *(continued)*

```
42      //Clean up
43
44      free(A);
45      free(B);
46      free(C);
47
48      cudaFree(A);
49      cudaFree(B);
50      cudaFree(C);
51
52    return 0;
53  }
54
55  __global__ vec_add(int *dA, int *dB, int *dC, int n)
56  {
57    int index = blockIdx.x*blockDim.x + threadIdx.x;
58
59    if( index < n)
60        C[index] = A[index] + B[index];
61  }
```

4.3.7 There Are Many More

The above discussion is not by any means an exhaustive list of parallel programming for heterogeneous systems. We would not be exaggerating if we said that there are new languages, or libraries, that appear almost every year. Of course we cannot go over all of them, or even most of them, here. But at least we get a flavor of how they work and how they differ in terms of portability, programmability, and performance.

There are some other models that are built with multicore in mind and not accelerators in general, unlike, say, CUDA and OpenCL. One very important model is threading building blocks(TBB).[7] It was developed by Intel as a C++ template library. The programmer's job is to break the computations, which are to be parallelized, into a group of tasks with dependencies, then schedule those tasks for execution. The runtime executes those tasks based on the dependencies of the multicore system. In order to ensure some kind of load balancing, TBB uses a work-stealing

---

7. https://www.threadingbuildingblocks.org/

strategy. That is, if a core finishes its assigned tasks, the runtime can assign another task from an overloaded core to that idle one. This makes programmability easy, yet not for free. The scheduling operation itself, done by the runtime, has its overhead. The runtime may not take into account the interconnect among cores and the heterogeneity in frequency when some cores become hot and hence slower due to DVFS, as we saw in Section 1.2.2.

Another important model is PThreads, or POSIX threads. Pthreads is a language-independent standard. That is, it can be implemented in any language to support multithreading parallel execution. There are many implementations in OS following the POSIX standard. It is important to note here that POSIX is not only about multithreading. It is a full standard for OS interfaces that are UNIX-like (e.g., Linux, FreeBSD, MAC, Android, etc.). This is why POSIX stands for "portable operating system interface." The Pthreads standard gives a lot of control to the programmer, at the expense of more coding, which means lower productivity from the programmer. All thread management, like creating, scheduling, and deleting threads, can be done by the application programmer. This has the advantage of less system calls and hence higher performance. Also, the fine-grain management of threads by the programmer allows for application-specific thread scheduling. Of course the situation is more complicated than this if we dig deeper. The programmer is aware of the threads, but these are user-level threads. The OS, the kernel, has its own threads of execution for any application. The relationship between user-level threads and kernel-level threads can be 1:1, N:1, or M:N depending on the implementation.

We will not go further here, but you get the idea. As a programmer for a heterogeneous system, you have a lot of choices. You pick what is beneficial to your application.

4.4 In Conclusion

This chapter has provided a quick tour of the most widely used languages in heterogeneous systems as well as a look at the psychology of programming. We did not cover everything, but we get the idea that we are still a long way to go from our programming language wish list. Let me try to summarize some challenges I see here.

- Programming languages are used by experts and novices alike. So, as we said earlier, a language must be able to abstract many things to be easy for programmers and increase productivity but also must support low-level tuning when needed. Most of the languages try to do this with varying degrees of success. So we are not there yet.

- Programming languages must be able to scale to a very large number of threads/processes. We are a few years away from exascale machines, and some problems do not manifest themselves except at large scale.

- Languages are pretty bad at dealing with reliability issues (e.g., transient errors). Soft errors are terrifying with large-scale machines.

- New programming models usually appear at computing inflection points. We are near exascale computing, which is probably the next inflection point, together with the Internet of Things (IoT). But do we really need new programming models? Or do we need to fix the ones we have? I believe we need collaboration between psychology and computer science on how programmers think and work.

Research Directions

In this last chapter we discuss the current trends in research affecting the design of parallel machines, which are now all heterogeneous machines.

5.1 Processing-in-Memory (PIM) / Near-Data Processing (NDP)

With communication cost and memory access cost skyrocketing relative to computation cost, moving processing to data instead of the other way around is gaining a lot of momentum, especially since the enabling technology is already there: 3D stacked memory and nonvolatile memory. PIM/NDP is currently a very hot topic of research with many interesting questions [Aga et al. 2017, Azarkhish et al. 2016, Balasubramonian et al. 2014, Boroumand et al. 2017, Loh et al. 2013, Punniyamurthy and Gerstlauer 2017, Seshadri et al. 2016, Siegl et al. 2016].

Think about something like matrix multiplication. Wouldn't it be more beneficial if it were done *in place* near the memory, or inside the memory, instead of moving a huge amount of data all the way up the memory hierarchy to the processor(s) to make a series of multiplications and additions? If the memory is equipped with a fused multiply-add engine, for example, then we would save a lot of bandwidth (a very scarce resource) and reduce cache access, which is translated to a better cache hit rate. However, the devil is in the details. Things are not very easy. There are a lot of open questions in this research area:

- What type of processing do we need to have in memory for current application trends?
- Do we need to have processing in the cache hierarchy? Why?
- How does NDP/PIM affect virtual memory?
- How does NDP/PIM affect programming models?
- How does NDP/PIM affect reliability and resilience of machines?
- Are there any security risks from using NPD/PIM?

NDP/PIM is the enabling technology for exascale computing.

5.2 Exascale Computing

A quick look at the Top500 supercomputers reavels that we are already at petascale computing. Exascale is the next big challenge. It is a much harder challenge than going from gigascale to petascale, and this is why its delivery deadline has been pushed several times. The most recent deadline is 2021. With exascale we can have way more realistic simulations of the human brain, analyzing the whole human genome very fast (curing cancer?), very fast scientific simulations pushing the frontiers of science. We can say that the potential is almost endless. So what is so challenging about getting to exascale? Here are the research challenges.

- If we just expanded the petascale machines to exascale, the power consumed would be prohibitive. The measure of success is 1 exaflop for 20–30 MW.

- What are the characteristics of a programming model for such a machine?

- How do we deal with silent and transient errors at that scale? Should they be exposed to programmers, complicating their task? Or should they be dealt with under the hood, consuming more power? (Look at the first item of this list.)

- Are our current algorithms scalable to that level?

- How can we scale the OS to deal with such a machine?

5.3 Neuromorphic Chips

Neuromorphic chips, or cognitive computing in general, are still not yet mainstream. But with many research groups working on it and many application ideas arising, we will soon see a neuromorphic coprocessor in a heterogeneous system. Before we proceed, we need to make an important distinction between two goals of neuromorphic chips. The first goal is to design a biological-like chip. In this case we are building a tool for neuroscientists to use. The other goal is to be *inspired* by the workings of the brain but design a chip that is useful for other cognitive applications, like pattern recognition, learning, etc. Given the nature of our book, we concentrate on the second goal.

Schuman et al. [2017] provides an almost exhaustive survey of advances in neuromorphic computing, with nearly 3000 references! Neuromorphic chips involve experience from many different fields, as shown in Figure 5.1. Neuroscientists formulate, and keep revising and refining, an accurate model for the human brain. Material engineers find the most efficient material—memristors, for example [Sayyaparaju et al. 2017, Shafiee et al. 2016]—to build chips inspired by that model. Electrical and computer engineers use the material and the model to de-

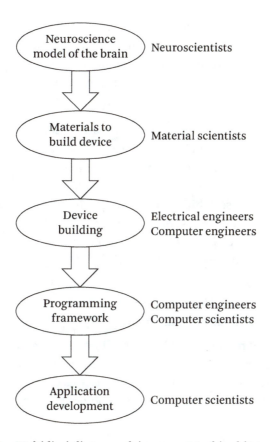

Figure 5.1   Multidisciplinary work in neuromorphic chip research.

sign the chip with the desired goals of speed, power, reliability, area, etc. They build the software framework to train and use those chips, to make it easier for application developers to use them. Finally, to be used efficiently in the outside world, application developers need to use those chips in their applications. The main reasons neuromorphic chips are attractive for applications related to pattern recognition, learning, prediction, etc. is their low power, speed, and higher reliability than programming the same machine learning algorithm on a traditional multicore processor.

Besides the above big picture about the ecosystem of neuromorphic chips, the research directions are related to (1) the neurons and their models, (2) modeling dendrites, axons, and synapses, if needed, to be as close as possible to the biological brain, (3) interconnection among neurons, (4) the learning algorithm and whether it is done online or offline, and (5) the hardware design itself. These directions are interrelated. For example, the design of the chip and neuron interconnection may dictate a specific learning algorithm or vice versa.

We summarize the most important research questions in the following list [US Department of Energy 2016].

- We are trying to build a hardware version of neurons, connected by synapses, with reconfigurable interconnections (or weights). What is the best technology? Is memristor the way to go? Or maybe some of the magnetic storage that we saw in Section 1.2, like MRAM, STTRAM, ReRAM, etc.? We need a technology with very high scalability and reconfigurability. Still open questions are, Which technology do we use? And what is the building block? To answer these questions, we need to decide on the type of processing done at each building block and how data are presented.

- Suppose we have continuously reconfigurable hardware. What does the computation model look like? This is totally different from what we are used to with fixed instruction sets and data paths.

- How will these neuromorphic chips learn? It is no longer a programming activity like what we are used to. At the same time we need a fast way to *teach* these chips or make them learn by themselves continuously. This may require interdisciplinary research, from psychology to neuroscience to computer science.

- To have wider applicability, neuromorphic chips must be easy to use. That is, easy to train. There is a need for a development environment to train/teach these chips that can abstract many of the lower-level issues from the user.

- How can we fit neuromorphic chips with other traditional chips, like multi-core and GPU, within the same computing ecosystem? The main challenge is that neuromorphic chip applications are still vague. Yes, we know they are good at recognition, categorization, etc. But what type of patterns? When do we decide to use those chips versus more traditional chips? The answer to these questions will become clearer as we use them in more and more applications and benchmark them against other approaches for different applications.

- A lot of work has been done on hardware support for machine learning. Can't we also use machine learning support for hardware? Instead of just using neuromorphic chips as coprocessors in a heterogeneous system to help in some operations, we can also use them to recognize any malfunction or performance degradation in the system and trigger correction actions.

5.4 Quantum Computing

Whenever a new hardware model appears, there is a big void between the application programmer and the machine itself. As time passes and people gain experience, the layers in between are filled up with compilers, low-level languages, high-level languages, workflows, etc. Quantum computers are in this early stage now. We are not yet at quantum supremacy (where traditional parallel machines cannot simulate that number of quantum bits (qubits)), but there are a lot of advances recently in that field. What type of programming languages do we need to have here? And how can they interact with programming models of traditional machines? Remember that a quantum computer is unlikely to be a stand-alone machine but rather a coprocessor in a large heterogeneous machine.

Even though research in quantum programming started as early as 1996, we still have a long way to go. We have to keep in mind that human intuition is better adapted to the classical world than the quantum world. Therefore, we can expect a lot of bugs and faults in designing quantum programs as compared to classical programs [Ying 2016].

Any program consists of two things: the data and the control that manipulates the data. In quantum computing, data are quantum (qubits). How about the control? Control can be classical, similar to what we have in traditional programs (e.g., loops, conditional, etc.). In that regard there has been some progress in classical control with quantum data. There is also quantum control (e.g., superposition), and quantum control with quantum data is still in its infancy. There is a lot of room for innovation and invention in the quantum world.

References

A. Abella and A. Gonzalez. June 2006. Heterogeneous way-size cache. In *International Conference on Supercomputing (ICS)*, pp. 239–248. DOI: 10.1145/1183401.1183436 33

A. Abualsamid. June 1998. PGP disk's security takes a bite out of crime. *Network Computing*, 9(10): 54. 47

O. Aciiçmez. 2007. Yet another microarchitectural attack: Exploiting i-cache. In *Proceedings of the 2007 ACM Workshop on Computer Security Architecture*, CSAW '07, pp. 11–18. ACM, New York. DOI: 10.1145/1314466.1314469 49

O. Aciiçmez, B. B. Brumley, and P. Grabher. 2010. New results on instruction cache attacks. In *Proceedings of the 12th International Conference on Cryptographic Hardware and Embedded Systems*, CHES '10, pp. 110–124. Springer-Verlag, Berlin, Heidelberg. 49

S. Aga, S. Jeloka, A. Subramaniyan, S. Narayanasamy, D. Blaauw, and R. Das. February 2017. Compute caches. In *23rd IEEE Symposium on High Performance Computer Architecture (HPCA)*. DOI: 10.1109/hpca.2017.21 91

A. Agarwal et al. 1988. An evaluation of directory schemes for cache coherence. In *25 Years ISCA: Retrospectives and Reprints*, pp. 353–362. DOI: 10.1145/633625.52432 34

A. Agarwal et al. 2004. Evaluating the raw microprocessor: An exposed-wire-delay architecture for ILP and streams. In *Proceedings of the 32nd International Symposium on Computer Architecture (ISCA)*, pp. 2–13. DOI: 10.1145/1028176.1006733 34

A. Agarwal and S. D. Pudar. 1993. Column-associative caches: A technique for reducing the miss rate of direct-mapped caches. In *Proceedings of the 20th International Symposium on Computer Architecture*, pp. 179–190. DOI: 10.1145/173682.165153 33

H. Al-Zoubi, A. Milenkovic, and M. Milenkovic. 2004. Performance evaluation of cache replacement policies for the SPEC CPU2000 benchmark suite. In *Proceedings of the 42nd ACM Southeast Conference*, pp. 267–272. DOI: 10.1145/986537.986601 35

D. H. Albonesi. 2002. Selective cache ways: On-demand cache resource allocation. *Journal of Instruction-Level Parallelism*, pp. 248–259. DOI: 10.1109/MICRO.1999.809463 33, 34

J. Allred, S. Roy, and K. Chakraborty. 2012. Designing for dark silicon: A methodological perspective on energy efficient systems. In *Proceedings of the 2012 ACM/IEEE International Symposium on Low Power Electronics and Design*, ISLPED '12, pp. 255–260. ACM, New York. DOI: 10.1145/2333660.2333720 3

J. Archibald and J.-L. Baer. May 1986. Cache coherence protocols: Evaluation using a multiprocessor simulation model. *ACM Transactions on Computer Systems*, pp. 273–298. DOI: 10.1145/6513.6514 34

E. Azarkhish, D. Rossi, I. Loi, and L. Benini. 2016. Design and evaluation of a processing-in-memory architecture for the smart memory cube. In *Proceedings of the 29th International Conference on Architecture of Computing Systems – ARCS 2016*, Volume 9637, pp. 19–31. Springer-Verlag, New York. DOI: 10.1007/978-3-319-30695-7_2 91

R. Balasubramonian, J. Chang, T. Manning, J. H. Moreno, R. Murphy, R. Nair, and S. Swanson. July 2014. Near-data processing: Insights from a micro-46 workshop. *IEE MICRO Magazine*, 34(4): 36–42. DOI: 10.1109/MM.2014.55 91

B. Beckmann and D. Wood. December 2004. Managing wire delay in large chip-multiprocessor caches. In *Proceedings of the 37th International Annual Symposium on Microarchitecture (Micro-37)*, pp. 319–330. DOI: 10.1109/MICRO.2004.21 34

L. Benini and G. DeMicheli. January 2002. Networks on chips: A new SoC paradigm. In *IEEE Computer*, pp. 70–78. DOI: 10.1109/2.976921 34

M. T. Billingsley III, B. R. Tibbitts, and A. D. George. 2010. Improving UPC productivity via integrated development tools. In *Proceedings of the Fourth Conference on Partitioned Global Address Space Programming Model*, PGAS '10, pp. 8:1–8:9. ACM, New York. DOI: 10.1145/2020373.2020381 68

S. Borkar, P. Dubey, K. Kahn, D. Kuck, H. Mulder, S. Pawlowski, and J. Rattner. 2006. Platform 2015: Intel processsor and platform evolution for the next decade. White paper, Intel Corporation. 35

A. Boroumand, S. Ghose, M. Patel, H. Hassan, B. Lucia, K. Hsieh, K. T. Malladi, H. Zheng, and O. Mutlu. January 2017. Lazypim: An efficient cache coherence mechanism for processing-in-memory. *IEEE Computer Architecture Letters*, 16(1): 46–50. DOI: 10.1109/LCA.2016.2577557 91

P. Bose. February 2013. Is dark silicon real? Technical perspective. *Communications of the ACM*, 56(2): 92–92. DOI: 10.1145/2408776.2408796 3

J. Boukhobza, S. Rubini, R. Chen, and Z. Shao. November 2017. Emerging NVM: A survey on architectural integration and research challenges. *ACM Transactions on Design Automation of Electronic Systems*, 23(2): 14:1–14:32. DOI: 10.1145/3131848 7

R. K. Braithwaite, W.-c. Feng, and P. S. McCormick. 2012. Automatic NUMA characterization using cbench. In *Proceedings of the 3rd ACM/SPEC International Conference on Performance Engineering*, ICPE '12, pp. 295–298. ACM, New York. DOI: 10.1145/2188286.2188342 6

S. Bratus, N. D'Cunha, E. Sparks, and S. W. Smith. 2008. Toctou, traps, and trusted computing. In *Proceedings of the 1st International Conference on Trusted Computing and Trust in Information Technologies: Trusted Computing—Challenges and Applications*, pp. 14–32. Springer-Verlag, Berlin, Heidelberg. DOI: 10.1007/978-3-540-68979-9_2 47

Broadcom Corporation, 2006. BCM1455: Quad-core 64-bit MIPS processor. http://www.broadcom.com/collateral/pb/1455-PB04-R.pdf. 35

B. Calder, D. Grunwald, and J. Emer. 1996. Predictive sequential associative cache. In *Proceedings of the 2nd International Symposium on High Performance Computer Architecture*, pp. 244–253. DOI: 10.1109/HPCA.1996.501190 33, 34

B. Calder, C. Krintz, S. John, and T. Austin. 1998. Cache-conscious data placement. In *Proceedings of the International Conference on Architecture Support for Programming Languages and Operating System (ASPLOS)*, pp. 139–149. 33

F. Cantonnet, Y. Yao, M. Zahran, and T. El-Ghazawi. April 2004. Productivity analysis of the UPC language. In *3rd International Workshop on Performance Modeling, Evaluation, and Optimization of Parallel and Distributed Systems (PMEO-PDS)*. DOI: 10.1109/IPDPS .2004.1303318 68

A. M. Caulfield, E. S. Chung, A. Putnam, H. Angepat, J. Fowers, M. Haselman, S. Heil, et al. 2016. A cloud-scale acceleration architecture. In *49th Annual IEEE/ACM International Symposium on Microarchitecture*, MICRO-49, pp. 7:1–7:13. IEEE Press, Piscataway, NJ. http://dl.acm.org/citation.cfm?id=3195638.3195647. 23

S. Chandrasekaran and G. Juckeland, eds. 2018. *OpenACC for Programmers: Concepts and Strategies*. Addison-Wesley, Boston, MA'. 83

J. Chang and G. S. Sohi. 2006. Cooperative caching for chip multiprocessors. In *Proceedings of the 33rd Annual International Symposium on Computer Architecture (ISCA)*, pp. 264–276. DOI: 10.1145/1150019.1136509 34

L. Cheng, N. Muralimanohar, K. Ramani, R. Balasubramonian, and J. Carter. June 2006. Interconnect-aware coherence protocols for chip multiprocessors. In *Proceedings of the 33rd IEEE/ACM International Symposium on Computer Architecture*, pp. 339–351. DOI: 10.1145/1150019.1136515 34

B. Childers, J. W. Davidson, and M. L. Soffa. 2003. Continuous compilation: A new approach to aggressive and adaptive code transformation. In *Proceedings of the 17th International Symposium on Parallel and Distributed Processing*, IPDPS '03, pp. 205–214. DOI: 10.1109/IPDPS.2003.1213375 71

Z. Chishti, M. D. Powell, and T. N. Vijaykumar. 2003. Distance associativity for high-performance energy-efficient non-uniform cache architectures. In *Proceedings of the 36th Annual IEEE/ACM International Symposium on Microarchitecture*, pp. 55–66. 6

J. Clark, S. Leblanc, and S. Knight. 2009. Hardware Trojan horse device based on unintended USB channels. In *Proceedings of the 2009 Third International Conference on Network and System Security*, NSS '09, pp. 1–8. IEEE Computer Society, Washington, DC. DOI: 10.1109/NSS.2009.48 49

J. Coburn, S. Ravi, A. Raghunathan, and S. Chakradhar. 2005. SECA: Security-enhanced communication architecture. In *Proceedings of the 2005 International Conference on Compilers, Architectures and Synthesis for Embedded Systems*, CASES '05, pp. 78–89. DOI: 10.1145/1086297.1086308 47

C. Cowan, C. Pu, D. Maier, H. Hinton, and J. Walpole. January 1998. StackGuard: Automatic adaptive detection and prevention of buffer-overflow attacks. In *Proceedings of the 7th USENIX Security Symposium*, pp. 63–78. 48

W. Dally and B. Towles. 2001. Route packets, not wires: On-chip interconnection networks. In *Proceedings of the 38th Conference on Design Automation*, pp.684–689. DOI: 10.1145/378239.379048 34

R. H. Dennard, F. H. Gaensslen, V. L. Rideout, E. Bassous, and A. R. LeBlanc. October 1974. Design of ion-implanted MOSFET's with very small physical dimensions. *IEEE Journal of Solid-State Circuits* 9(5): 256–268. DOI: 10.1109/JSSC.1974.1050511 2

R. V. der Pas, E. Stotzer, and C. Terboven. 2017. *Using OpenMP—the Next Step*. MIT Press, Cambridge, MA. 77

A. S. Dhodapkar and J. E. Smith. 2002. Managing multi-configuration hardware via dynamic working set analysis. In *Proceedings of the 17th International Symposium on Computer Architecture*, pp. 233–244. DOI: 10.1145/545214.545241 33

G. Di Crescenzo. 2005. Security of erasable memories against adaptive adversaries. In *Proceedings of theedings of the 2005 ACM Workshop on Storage Security and Survivability*, StorageSS '05, pp. 115–122. DOI: 10.1145/1103780.1103798 47

S. J. Eggers and R. H. Katz. 1989. Evaluating the performance of four snooping cache coherence protocols. In *Proceedings of the 22nd Annual International Symposium on Computer Architecture*, pp. 2–15. DOI: 10.1145/74926.74927 34

M. Ekman, F. Dahlgren, and P. Stenström. August 2002. TLB and snoop energy-reduction using virtual caches for low-power chip-multiprocessor. In *Proceedings of the IEEE/ACM International Symposium on Low Power Electronics and Design*, pp. 243–246. DOI: 10.1145/566408.566471 34

R. Elbaz, L. Torres, G. Sassatelli, P. Guillemin, C. Anguille, M. Bardouillet, C. Buatois, and J. B. Rigaud. 2005. Hardware engines for bus encryption: A survey of existing techniques. In *Proceedings of the Conference on Design, Automation and Test in Europe*, DATE '05, Volume 3, pp. 40–45. DOI: 10.1109/DATE.2005.170 47

H. Esmaeilzadeh, E. Blem, R. St. Amant, K. Sankaralingam, and D. Burger. 2011. Dark silicon and the end of multicore scaling. In *Proceedings of the 38th Annual International Symposium on Computer Architecture*, ISCA '11, pp. 365–376. ACM, New York. DOI: 10.1145/2000064.2000108 3

K. I. Farkas, P. Chow, N. P. Jouppi, and Z. Vranesic. 1997. The multicluster architecture: Reducing cycle time through partitioning. In *Proceedings of the 30th International Symposium on Microarchitecture*, pp. 149–159. DOI: 10.1023/A:1018782806674 34

F. Fiori and F. Musolino. 2001. Analysis of EME produced by a microcontroller operation. In *Proceedings of the Conference on Design, Automation and Test in Europe*, DATE '01, pp. 341–347. IEEE Press, Piscataway, NJ. DOI: 10.1109/DATE.2001.915047 49

A. Fiskiran and R. Lee. October 2004. Runtime execution monitoring (REM) to detect and prevent malicious code execution. In *Proceedings of the IEEE International Conference on Computer Design*, pp. 452–457. DOI: 10.1109/ICCD.2004.1347961 49

K. Flautner, N. Kim, S. Martin, D. Blaauw, and T. Mudge. May 2002. Drowsy caches: Simple techniques for reducing leakage power. In *Proceedings of the Annual International Symposium on Computer Architecture*, pp. 147–157. DOI: 10.1145/545214.545232 34

K. Gandolfi, C. Mourtel, and F. Olivier. 2001. Electromagnetic analysis: Concrete results. In *Proceedings of the Third International Workshop on Cryptographic Hardware and Embedded Systems*, CHES '01, pp. 251–261. Springer-Verlag, London. DOI: 10.1007/3-540-44709-1_21 49

B. Gassend, G. E. Suh, D. Clarke, M. V. Dijk, and S. Devadas. 2003. Caches and hash trees for efficient memory integrity verification. In *9th International Symposium on High Performance Computer Architecture*, pp. 295–306. DOI: 10.1109/HPCA.2003.1183547 49

O. Gelbart, P. Ott, B. Narahari, R. Simha, A. Choudhary, and J. Zambreno. May 2005. CODESSEAL: Compiler/FPGA approach to secure applications. In *Proceedings of the IEEE International Conference on Intelligence and Security Informatics*, pp. 530–535. DOI: 10.1007/11427995_54 49

K. Ghose and M. Kamble. August 1999. Reducing power in superscalar processor caches using subbanking, multiple line buffers and bit-line segmentation. In *Proceedings of the IEEE/ACM International Symposium on Low Power Electronics and Design*, pp. 70–75. DOI: 10.1145/313817.313860 34

B. Grigorian, N. Farahpour, and G. Reinman. February 2015. Brainiac: Bringing reliable accuracy into neurally-implemented approximate computing. In *High Performance Computer Architecture (HPCA), 2015 IEEE 21st International Symposium*, pp. 615–626. DOI: 10.1109/HPCA.2015.7056067 26

F. Guo and Y. Solihin. June 2006. An analytical model for cache replacement policy performance. In *SIGMETRICS '06/Performance '06: Proceedings of the Joint International Conference on Measurement and Modeling of Computer Systems*, pp. 228–239. DOI: 10.1145/1140103.1140304 35

Y. Guo, Q. Zhuge, J. Hu, J. Yi, M. Qiu, and E. H.-M. Sha. June 2013. Data placement and duplication for embedded multicore systems with scratch pad memory. *IEEE Transactions on Computer-Aided Design of Integrated Circuits and Systems*, 32(6): 809–817. DOI: 10.1109/TCAD.2013.2238990 35

L. Hammond, B. Nayfeh, and K. Olukotun. 1997. A single-chip multiprocessor. *IEEE Computer*, pp. 79–85. DOI: 10.1109/2.612253 34

T. D. Han and T. S. Abdelrahman. 2011. Reducing branch divergence in GPU programs. In *Proceedings of the Fourth Workshop on General Purpose Processing on Graphics Processing Units*, GPGPU-4, pp. 3:1–3:8. ACM, New York. DOI: 10.1145/1964179.1964184 22

K. Hazelwood. 2011. *Dynamic Binary Modification: Tools, Techniques, and Applications*. Morgan & Claypool Publishers, San Rafael, CA. 71

N. Hemsoth and T. P. Morgan. 2017. *FPGA Frontiers: New Applications in Reconfigurable Computing*. Next Platform Press, High Point, NC. 23

J.-M. Hoc, ed. 1990. *Psychology of Programming*, 1. Elsevier, New York. 69

R. Huang, D. Y. Deng, and G. E. Suh. March 2010. Orthrus efficient software integrity protection on multi-cores. In *Proceedings of the International Conference on*

Architectural Support for Programming Languages and Operating Systems, pp. 371–384. DOI: 10.1145/1736020.1736062 49

G. F. Hughes and J. F. Murray. February 2005. Reliability and security of RAID storage systems and D2D archives using SATA disk drives. In *IEEE Transactions on Storage*, 1(1): 95–107. DOI: 10.1145/1044956.1044961 47

W. W. Hwu. 2015. *Heterogeneous System Architecture: A New Compute Platform Infrastructure*, 1. Morgan Kaufmann, Burlington, MA. 85

K. Inoue, V. Moshnyaga, and K. Murakami. February 2002. Trends in high-performance, low-power cache memory architectures. *IEICE Transactions on Electronics*, E85-C(2): 303–314. 34

T. B. Jablin, P. Prabhu, J. A. Jablin, N. P. Johnson, S. R. Beard, and D. I. August. 2011. Automatic CPU-GPU communication management and optimization. In *Proceedings of the 32nd ACM SIGPLAN Conference on Programming Language Design and Implementation*, PLDI '11, pp. 142–151. DOI: 10.1145/1993498.1993516 19

A. Jaleel, W. Hasenplaugh, M. Qureshi, J. Sebot, S. Steely, and J. Emer. 2008. Adaptive insertion policies for managing shared caches. In *PACT '08: Proceedings of the 17th International Conference on Parallel Architectures and Compilation Techniques*, pp. 208–219. DOI: 10.1145/1454115.1454145 51

A. Jaleel, J. Nuzman, A. Moga, S. Steely, and J. Emer. February 2015. High performing cache hierarchies for server workloads: Relaxing inclusion to capture the latency benefits of exclusive caches. In *High Performance Computer Architecture (HPCA), 2015 IEEE 21st International Symposium*, pp. 343–353. DOI: 10.1109/HPCA.2015.7056045 51

J. Jeong and M. Dubois. February 2003. Cost-sensitive cache replacement algorithms. In *Proceedings of the 9th IEEE Symposium on High Performance Computer Architecture*, pp. 327–337. DOI: 10.1109/HPCA.2003.1183550 35, 51

N. E. Jerger, T. Krishna, and L.-S. Peh. 2017. *On-Chip Networks*. Morgan & Claypool Publishers, San Rafael, CA. 36

Y. Jin, N. Kupp, and Y. Makris. 2009. Experiences in hardware Trojan design and implementation. In *Proceedings of the 2009 IEEE International Workshop on Hardware-Oriented Security and Trust*, HST '09, pp. 50–57. IEEE Computer Society, Washington, DC. DOI: 10.1109/HST.2009.5224971 49

N. P. Jouppi, C. Young, N. Patil, D. Patterson, G. Agrawal, R. Bajwa, S. Bates, et al. 2017. In-datacenter performance analysis of a tensor processing unit. In *Proceedings of the 44th Annual International Symposium on Computer Architecture*, ISCA '17, pp. 1–12. ACM, New York. DOI: 10.1145/3079856.3080246 27

D. R. Kaeli, P. Mistry, D. Schaa, and D. P. Zhang. 2015. *Heterogeneous Computing with OpenCL 2.0*, 3. Morgan Kaufmann, Burlington, MA. 78

M. Kamble and K. Ghose. August 1997. Analytical energy dissipation models for low power caches. In *Proceedings of the IEEE/ACM International Symposium on Low Power Electronics and Design*, pp. 143–148. DOI: 10.1145/263272.263310 34

S. Kang, H. J. Choi, C. H. Kim, S. W. Chung, D. Kwon, and J. C. Na. 2011. Exploration of CPU/GPU co-execution: From the perspective of performance, energy, and temperature. In *Proceedings of the 2011 ACM Symposium on Research in Applied Computation*, RACS '11, pp. 38–43. DOI: 10.1145/2103380.2103388 17

T. Karkhanis and J. E. Smith. June 2002. A day in the life of a data cache miss. In *Proceedings of the 2nd Annual Workshop on Memory Performance Issues (WMPI)*. 33

R. Karri, J. Rajendran, K. Rosenfeld, and M. Tehranipoor. 2010. Trustworthy hardware: Identifying and classifying hardware Trojans. *Computer*, 43: 39–46. DOI: 10.1109/MC .2010.299 47, 49

R. Karri, K. Wu, P. Mishra, and Y. Kim. 2001. Concurrent error detection of fault-based side-channel cryptanalysis of 128-bit symmetric block ciphers. In *Proceedings of the 38th annual Design Automation Conference*, DAC '01, pp. 579–584. ACM, New York. DOI: 10.1145/378239.379027 49

S. Kaxiras, Z. Hu, and M. Martonosi. June 2001. Cache decay: Exploiting generational behavior to reduce cache leakage power. In *Proceedings of the 28th IEEE/ACM International Symposium on Computer Architecture*, pp. 240–251. DOI: 10.1145/384285 .379268 34

G. S. Kc, A. D. Keromytis, and V. Prevelakis. 2003. Countering code-injection attacks with instruction-set randomization. In *Proceedings of the 10th ACM Conference on Computer and Communications Security*, CCS '03, pp. 272–280. ACM, New York. DOI: 10.1145/ 948109.948146 48

M. Kharbutli and Y. Solihin. October 2005. Counter-based cache replacement algorithms. In *Proceedings of the International Conference on Computer Design*, pp. 61–68. DOI: 10.1109/ICCD.2005.41 51

H. Kim, N. Vijaykrishnan, M. Kandemir, A. Sivasubramaniam, M. Irwin, and E. Geethanjali. August 2001. Power-aware partitioned cache architectures. In *Proceedings of the IEEE/ACM International Symposium on Low Power Electronics and Design*, pp. 64–67. DOI: 10.1145/383082.383095 34

J. Kim, W. J. Dally, S. Scott, and D. Abts. 2008. Technology-driven, highly-scalable dragonfly topology. In *Proceedings of the 35th Annual International Symposium on Computer Architecture*, ISCA '08, pp. 77–88. IEEE Computer Society, Washington, DC. DOI: 10.1109/ISCA.2008.19 41

N. Kim, K. Flautner, D. Blaauw, and T. Mudge. November 2002. Drowsy instruction caches: Leakage power reduction using dynamic voltage scaling and cache sub-bank prediction. In *Proceedings of the IEEE/ACM 35th International Symposium on Microarchitecture*, pp. 219–230. DOI: 10.1109/MICRO.2002.1176252 34

N. Kim, K. Flautner, D. Blaauw, and T. Mudge. February 2004a. Circuit and microarchitectural techniques for reducing cache leakage power. *IEEE Transactions on VLSI* 12(2): 167–184. DOI: 10.1109/TVLSI.2003.821550 34

S. Kim, D. Chandra, and Y. Solihin. 2004b. Fair cache sharing and partitioning in a chip multiprocessor architecture. In *PACT '04: Proceedings of the 13th International*

Conference on Parallel Architectures and Compilation Techniques, pp. 111–122. DOI: 10.1109/PACT.2004.15 34

J. Kin, M. Gupta, and W. H. Mangione-Smith. 1997. The filter cache: An energy efficient memory structure. In *Proceedings of the 30th Annual International Symposium on Microarchitecture (MICRO-30)*, pp. 184–193. DOI: 10.1109/MICRO.1997.645809 33

M. J. Kobrinsky, B. A. Block, J.-F. Zheng, B. C. Barnett, E. Mohammed, M. Reshotko, F. Robinson, S. List, I. Young, and K. Cadien. May 2004. On-chip optical interconnects. *Intel Technology Journal*, 8(2): 129–142. 39

A. K. Kodi and A. Louri. March 2007. Power-aware bandwidth-reconfigurable optical interconnects for high-performance computing (HPC) systems. In *IEEE Parallel and Distributed Processing Symposium*. IPDPS 2007, pp. 1–10. DOI: 10.1109/IPDPS .2007.370273 39

J. Kong, O. Aciicmez, J.-P. Seifert, and H. Zhou. 2008. Deconstructing new cache designs for thwarting software cache-based side channel attacks. In *Proceedings of the 2nd ACM Workshop on Computer Security Architectures*, CSAW '08, pp. 25–34. ACM, New York. DOI: 10.1145/1456508.1456514 49

P. Kongetira, K. Aingaran, and K. Olukotun. March 2005. Niagara: A 32-way multithreaded SPARC processor. *IEEE Micro*, 25(2): 21–29. DOI: 10.1109/MM.2005.35 35

V. Krishnan and J. Torrellas. 1999. A chip-multiprocessor architecture with speculative multithreading. *IEEE Transactions on Computers*, 48(9): 866–880. DOI: 10.1109/ 12.795218 34

R. Kumar, V. Zyuban, and D. Tullsen. June 2005. Interconnection in multi-core architectures: Understanding mechanisms, overheads, and scaling. In *International Symposium on Computer Architecture*, pp. 408–419. DOI: 10.1109/ISCA.2005.34 36

G. Kurian, J. E. Miller, J. Psota, J. Eastep, J. Liu, J. Michel, L. C. Kimerling, and A. Agarwal. 2010. Atac: A 1000-core cache-coherent processor with on-chip optical network. In *Proceedings of the 19th International Conference on Parallel Architectures and Compilation Techniques*, PACT '10, pp. 477–488. ACM, New York. DOI: 10.1145/ 1854273.1854332 39

H. Lee, G. Tyson, and M. Farrens. December 2000. Eager writeback—a technique for improving bandwidth utilization. In *Proceedings of the IEEE/ACM 33nd International Symposium on Microarchitecture*, pp. 11–21. DOI: 10.1145/360128.360132 60

J.-H. Lee and S.-D. Kim. 2002. Application-adaptive intelligent cache memory system. *ACM Transactions on Embedded Computing Systems*, 1(1): 56–78. DOI: 10.1145/581888 .581893 33

R. B. Lee, D. K. Karig, J. P. McGregor, and Z. Shi. March 2003. Enlisting hardware architecture to thwart malicious code injection. In *Proceedings of the International Conference on Security in Pervasive Computing*, pp. 237–252. DOI: 10.1007/978-3-540-39881-3_21 48

J. Lin. 2008. On malicious software classification. In *Proceedings of the 2008 International Symposium on Intelligent Information Technology Application Workshops*, pp. 368–371.

IEEE Computer Society, Washington, DC. DOI: 10.1109/IITA.Workshops.2008.106
47

J. L. Lo, J. S. Emer, H. M. Levy, R. L. Stamm, and D. M. Tullsen. 1997. Converting thread-level parallelism to instruction-level parallelism via simultaneous multithreading. *ACM Transactions on Computer Systems*, 15(3): 322–354. DOI: 10.1145/263326.263382 3, 35

G. H. Loh, N. Jayasena, M. Oskin, M. Nutter, D. Roberts, M. R. Meswani, D. P. Zhang, and M. Ignatowski. 2013. A processing-in-memory taxonomy and a case for studying fixed-function PIM. *1st Workshop on Near Data Processing*, held in conjunction with the *46th IEEE/ACM International Symposium on Microarchitecture (MICRO 46)*. 91

D. McGinn-Combs. February 2007. Security architecture and models. http://www.giac.org/resources. 47

N. Megiddo and D. s. Modha, 2004. Outperforming LRU with an Adaptive Replacement Cache Algorithm. *Computer* 37(4): 58–65. DOI: 10.1109/MC.2004.1297303 35

D. S. Modha, R. Ananthanarayanan, S. K. Esser, A. Ndirango, A. J. Sherbondy, and R. Singh. August 2011. Cognitive computing. *Communications of the ACM*, 54(8): 62–71. DOI: 10.1145/1978542.1978559 25

G. E. Moore. April 1965. Cramming more components onto integrated circuits. *Electronics*, pp. 114–117. 2

A. Moshovos. June 2005. Regionscout: Exploiting coarse grain sharing in snoop-based coherence. In *Proceedings of the 32nd IEEE/ACM International Symposium on Computer Architecture*, pp. 234–245. DOI: 10.1109/ISCA.2005.42 34

B. A. Nayfeh. 1998. The case for a single-chip multiprocessor. PhD thesis, Stanford University, Stanford, CA. 34

Nergal. December 2001. Advanced return-into-lib(c) exploits (PaX case study). http://www.phrack.org/. 48

M. Nijim, X. Qin, and T. Xie. November 2006. Modeling and improving security of a local disk system for write-intensive workloads. *ACM Transactions on Storage*, 2(4): 400–423. DOI: 10.1145/1210596.1210598 47

C. J. Nitta, M. K. Farrens, and V. Akella. 2013. *On-Chip Photonic Interconnects: A Computer Architect's Perspective*. Morgan & Claypool Publishers, San Rafael, CA. 39

NVIDIA, 2017. NVIDIA Tesla v100 GPU architecture. http://images.nvidia.com/content/volta-architecture/pdf/volta-architecture-whitepaper.pdf 19

K. Patel and S. Parameswaran. June 2008. SHIELD: A software hardware design methodology for security and reliability of MPSoCs. In *Proceedings of the ACM/IEEE Design Automation Conference*, pp. 858–861. DOI: 10.1145/1391469.1391686 50

J.-K. Peir, W. Hsu, H. Young, and S. Ong. 1996. Improving cache performance with balanced tag and data paths. In *Proceedings of the International Conference on Architecture Support for Programming Languages and Operating Systems (ASPLOS)*, pp. 268–278. DOI: 10.1145/237090.237202 34

J.-K. Peir, Y. Lee, and W. Hsu. 1998. Capturing dynamic memory reference behavior with adaptive cache toplogy. In *Proceedings of the International Conference on Architecture*

Support for Programming Languages and Operating Systems (ASPLOS), pp. 240–250. DOI: 10.1145/291006.291053 33

G. Pekhimenko, T. Huberty, R. Cai, O. Mutlu, P. Gibbons, M. Kozuch, and T. Mowry. February 2015. Exploiting compressed block size as an indicator of future reuse. In *High Performance Computer Architecture (HPCA), 2015 IEEE 21st International Symposium*, pp. 51–63. DOI: 10.1109/HPCA.2015.7056021 35

M. Potkonjak, A. Nahapetian, M. Nelson, and T. Massey. 2009. Hardware Trojan horse detection using gate-level characterization. In *Proceedings of the 46th Annual Design Automation Conference*, DAC '09, pp. 688–693. ACM, New York. DOI: 10.1145/1629911 .1630091 49

S. M. Potter. 2001. What can artificial intelligence get from neuroscience? In *Artificial Intelligence Festschrift: The Next 50 Years*, pp. 174–185. Springer-Verlag, New York. 26

K. Punniyamurthy and A. Gerstlauer. 2017. Exploring non-uniform processing in-memory architectures. In *1st Workshop on Hardware/Software Techniques for Minimizing Data Movement*, held in conjunction with PACT. 91

M. Qureshi, A. Jaleel, Y. Patt, S. C. Steely, and J. Emer. June 2007. Adaptive insertion policies for high performance caching. In *Proceedings of the 34th International Symposium on Computer Architecture (ISCA)*, pp. 381–391. DOI: 10.1145/1250662.1250709 51, 60

M. Qureshi, D. Lynch, O. Mutlu, and Y. Patt. June 2006. A case for MLP-aware cache replacement. In *Proceedings of the 33rd International Symposium on Computer Architecture (ISCA)*, pp. 167–178. DOI: 10.1109/ISCA.2006.5 35, 51

M. K. Qureshi and Y. N. Patt. 2006. Utility-based cache partitioning: A low-overhead, high-performance, runtime mechanism to partition shared caches. In *Proceedings of the 39th Annual IEEE/ACM International Symposium on Microarchitecture*, pp. 423–432. DOI: 10.1109/MICRO.2006.49 34

R. Ramanathan. 2006. Intel multi-core processors: Making the move to quad-core and beyond. White paper, Intel Corporation. 35

J. Reineke, D. Grund, C. Berg, and R. Wilhelm. September 2006. Predictability of cache replacement policies. Reports of SFB/TR 14 AVACS 9, SFB/TR 14 AVACS. http://www.avacs.org 35

A. Ros, M. Davari, and S. Kaxiras. February 2015. Hierarchical private/shared classification: The key to simple and efficient coherence for clustered cache hierarchies. In *High Performance Computer Architecture (HPCA), 2015 IEEE 21st International Symposium*, pp. 186–197. DOI: 10.1109/HPCA.2015.7056032 35

X. Ruan, A. Manzanares, S. Yin, M. Nijim, and X. Qin. 2009. Can we improve energy efficiency of secure disk systems without modifying security mechanisms? In *Proceedings of the 2009 IEEE International Conference on Networking, Architecture, and Storage*, NAS '09, pp. 413–420. DOI: 10.1109/NAS.2009.71 47

K. Rupp. 2018. 42 years of microprocessor trend data. https://github.com/karlrupp/ microprocessor-trend-data (last accessed March 2018). 2

S. K. Sadasivam, B. W. Thompto, R. Kalla, and W. J. Starke. March 2017. IBM power9 processor architecture. *IEEE Micro*, 37(2): 40–51. DOI: 10.1109/MM.2017.40 15

S. Sayyaparaju, G. Chakma, S. Amer, and G. S. Rose. 2017. Circuit techniques for online learning of memristive synapses in CMOS-memristor neuromorphic systems. In *Proceedings of the Great Lakes Symposium on VLSI 2017*, GLSVLSI '17, pp. 479–482. ACM, New York. DOI: 10.1145/3060403.3060418 26, 92

M. Schuette and J. Shen. March 1987. Processor control flow monitoring using signatured instruction streams. *IEEE Transactions on Computers*, C-36(3): 264–276. DOI: 10.1109/TC.1987.1676899 49

C. D. Schuman, T. E. Potok, R. M. Patton, J. D. Birdwell, M. E. Dean, G. S. Rose, and J. S. Plank. May 2017. A survey of neuromorphic computing and neural networks in hardware. *ArXiv e-prints*. https://arxiv.org/abs/1705.06963 92

V. Seshadri, D. Lee, T. Mullins, H. Hassan, A. Boroumand, J. Kim, M. A. Kozuch, O. Mutlu, P. B. Gibbons, and T. C. Mowry. 2016. Buddy-RAM: Improving the performance and efficiency of bulk bitwise operations using DRAM. https://arxiv.org/abs/1611.09988 91

A. Shafiee, A. Nag, N. Muralimanohar, R. Balasubramonian, J. P. Strachan, M. Hu, R. S. Williams, and V. Srikumar. 2016. Isaac: A convolutional neural network accelerator with in-situ analog arithmetic in crossbars. In *Proceedings of the 43rd International Symposium on Computer Architecture*, ISCA '16, pp. 14–26. IEEE Press, Piscataway, NJ. DOI: 10.1109/ISCA.2016.12 92

R. Sheikh and M. Kharbutli. October 2010. Improving cache performance by combining cost-sensitivity and locality principles in cache replacement algorithms. In *Proceedings of the International Conference on Computer Design (ICCD)*, pp. 76–83. DOI: 10.1109/ICCD.2010.5647594 51

P. Siegl, R. Buchty, and M. Berekovic. 2016. Data-centric computing frontiers: A survey on processing-in-memory. In *Proceedings of the Second International Symposium on Memory Systems*, MEMSYS '16, pp. 295–308. ACM, New York. DOI: 10.1145/2989081.2989087 91

B. Sinharoy, R. N. Kalla, J. M. Tendler, R. J. Eickemeyer, and J. B. Joyner. 2005. Power5 system microarchitecture. *IBM Journal of Research and Development*, 49(4/5): 505–521. DOI: 10.1147/rd.494.0505 35

A. Smith. 1982. Cache memories. *ACM Computing Surveys*, 14(3): 473–530. 33

F.-X. Standaert, T. G. Malkin, and M. Yung. 2009. A unified framework for the analysis of side-channel key recovery attacks. In *Proceedings of the 28th Annual International Conference on Advances in Cryptology: The Theory and Applications of Cryptographic Techniques*, EUROCRYPT '09, pp. 443–461. Springer-Verlag, Berlin, Heidelberg, pp. 443–461. DOI: 10.1007/978-3-642-01001-9_26 47, 49

L. Su, S. Courcambeck, P. Guillemin, C. Schwarz, and R. Pacalet. 2009. SecBus: Operating system controlled hierarchical page-based memory bus protection. In *Proceedings of the Conference on Design, Automation and Test in Europe*, DATE '09, pp. 570–573. DOI: 10.1109/DATE.2009.5090729 47

H. Sutter. March 2005. The free lunch is over: A fundamental turn toward concurrency in software. *Dr. Dobb's Journal*, 30(3): 202–210. 4

TCG. April 2008. Trusted platform module (TPM) summary. http://www.trustedcomputinggroup.org/. 47

M. Tehranipoor and F. Koushanfar. January 2010. A survey of hardware Trojan taxonomy and detection. *IEEE Design & Test of Computers*, 27(1): 10–25. DOI: 10.1109/MDT.2010.7 49

A. Tereshkin. 2010. Evil maid goes after PGP whole disk encryption. In *Proceedings of the 3rd International Conference on Security of Information and Networks*, SIN '10, p. 2. ACM, New York. DOI: 10.1145/1854099.1854103 49

K. Tiri. 2007. Side-channel attack pitfalls. In *Proceedings of the 44th Annual Design Automation Conference*, DAC '07, pp. 15–20. ACM, New York. DOI: 10.1145/1278480.1278485 47, 49

M. Tomasevic and V. Milutinovic. 1993. *The Cache Coherence Problem in Shared-Memory Multiprocessors: Hardware Solutions*. IEEE Computer Society Press, Los Alamitos, CA. 34

D. M. Tullsen, S. Eggers, and H. M. Levy. 1995. Simultaneous multithreading: Maximizing on-chip parallelism. In *Proceedings of the 22nd International Symposium on Computer Architecture*, pp. 392–403. DOI: 10.1109/ISCA.1995.524578 3, 14, 34, 35

D. Unat, A. Dubey, T. Hoefler, J. Shalf, M. Abraham, M. Bianco, B. L. Chamberlain, et al. October 2017. Trends in data locality abstractions for HPC systems. *IEEE Transactions on Parallel and Distributed Systems*, 20(10): 3007–3020. DOI: 10.1109/TPDS.2017 .2703149 64

US Department of Energy. April 2013. Technical challenges of exascale computing. Technical Report JSR-12-310. https://fas.org/irp/agency/dod/jason/exascale.pdf.

US Department of Energy. 2016. Neuromorphic computing, architectures, models, and applications: A beyond-CMOS approach to future computing. Technical report, Oak Ridge National Laboratory. 94

A. S. Vaidya, A. Shayesteh, D. H. Woo, R. Saharoy, and M. Azimi. 2013. SIMD divergence optimization through intra-warp compaction. In *Proceedings of the 40th Annual International Symposium on Computer Architecture*, ISCA '13, pp. 368–379. ACM, New York. DOI: 10.1145/2485922.2485954 22

K. Varadarajan, S. Nandy, V. Sharda, A. Bharadwaj, R. Iyer, S. Makineni, and D. Newell. June 2006. Molecular caches: A caching structure for dynamic creation of application-specific heterogeneous cache regions. In *Proceedings of the 39th Annual IEEE/ACM International Symposium on Microarchitecture (MICRO-39)*, pp. 433–442. DOI: 10.1109/MICRO.2006.38 34

R. Vaslin, G. Gogniat, J.-P. Diguet, E. Wanderley, R. Tessier, and W. Burleson. February 2009. A security approach for off-chip memory in embedded microprocessor systems.

Microprocessors and Microsystems, 33(1): 37–45. DOI: 10.1016/j.micpro.2008.08.008 47

A. V. Veidenbaum, W. Tang, R. Gupta, A. Nicolau, and X. Ji. 1999. Adapting cache line size to application behavior. In *Proceedings of the 1999 International Conference on Supercomputing*, pp. 145–154. DOI: 10.1145/305138.305188 33, 34

A. Waksman and S. Sethumadhavan. 2010. Tamper evident microprocessors. In *Proceedings of the 2010 IEEE Symposium on Security and Privacy*, SP '10, pp. 173–188. IEEE Computer Society, Washington, DC. DOI: 10.1109/SP.2010.19 47, 49

K. Wang, K. Angstadt, C. Bo, N. Brunelle, E. Sadredini, T. Tracy II, J. Wadden, M. Stan, and K. Skadron. 2016. An overview of Micron's automata processor. In *Proceedings of the Eleventh IEEE/ACM/IFIP International Conference on Hardware/Software Codesign and System Synthesis*, CODES '16, pp. 14:1–14:3. ACM, New York. DOI: 10.1145/2968456 .2976763 24

P. Wang, D. Feng, W. Wu, and L. Zhang. 2009. On the correctness of an approach against side-channel attacks. In *Proceedings of the 5th International Conference on Information Security Practice and Experience*, ISPEC '09, pp. 336–344. Springer-Verlag, Berlin, Heidelberg. 47, 49

X. Wang, H. Salmani, M. Tehranipoor, and J. Plusquellic. 2008. Hardware Trojan detection and isolation using current integration and localized current analysis. In *Proceedings of the 2008 IEEE International Symposium on Defect and Fault Tolerance of VLSI Systems*, pp. 87–95. IEEE Computer Society, Washington, DC. DOI: 10.1109/DFT.2008.61 49

E. Wheeler. September 2008. Replay attacks. http://www.sans.org/. 48

W. Wong and J.-L. Baer. January 2000. Modified LRU policies for improving second level cache behavior. In *Sixth International Symposium on High-Performance Computer Architecture (HPCA-6)*, pp. 49–60. DOI: 10.1109/ HPCA.2000.824338 35

S. C. Woo, M. Ohara, E. Torrie, J. P. Singh, and A. Gupta. 1995. The SPLASH-2 programs: Characterization and methodological considerations. In *Proceedings of the 22nd Annual International Symposium on Computer Architecture*, ISCA '95, pp. 24–36. ACM, New York. DOI: 10.1145/223982.223990 51

X. Xie, Y. Liang, Y. Wang, G. Sun, and T. Wang. February 2015. Coordinated static and dynamic cache bypassing for GPUs. In *High Performance Computer Architecture (HPCA), 2015 IEEE 21st International Symposium on*, pp. 76–88. DOI: 10.1109/HPCA .2015.7056023 35

J. Xue, A. Garg, B. Ciftcioglu, J. Hu, S. Wang, I. Savidis, M. Jain, et al. 2010. An intra-chip free-space optical interconnect. In *Proceedings of the 37th Annual International Symposium on Computer Architecture*, ISCA '10, pp. 94–105. ACM, New York. DOI: 10.1145/1815961.1815975 39

C. Yan, D. Englender, M. Prvulovic, B. Rogers, and Y. Solihin. 2006. Improving cost, performance, and security of memory encryption and authentication. In *Proceedings of the 33rd Annual International Symposium on Computer Architecture*, ISCA '06, pp. 179–190. DOI: 10.1145/1150019.1136502 47

H. Yang, R. Govindarajan, G. R. Gao, and Z. Hu. December 2005. Improving power efficiency with compiler-assisted cache replacement. *Journal of Embedded Computing*, 1(4): 487–499. 51

T. T. Ye. 2003. Physical planning for on-chip multiprocessor networks and switch fabrics. In *14th IEEE International Conference on Application-Specific Systems, Architectures and Processors (ASAP'03)*, pp. 97–107. DOI: 10.1109/ASAP.2003.1212833 34

M. Ying. 2016. *Foundations of Quantum Programming*, 1. Morgan Kaufmann, Burlingon, MA. 95

M. Zahran. March 2016. Brain-inspired machines: What, exactly, are we looking for? *IEEE Pulse*, 7(2): 48–51. DOI: 10.1109/MPUL.2015.2513728 26

W. Zhang, M. Kandemir, M. Karakoy, and G. Chen. August 2005. Reducing data cache leakage energy using a compiler-based approach. *ACM Transactions on Embedded Computing Systems*, 4(3): 652–678. DOI: 10.1145/1086519.1086529

Index

3D stacked memory, 22

Altera, 24
AMD, 14, 18, 45
AMD Opteron, 45
application-specific integrated circuit, 23
Arm, 30, 31
artificial intelligence, 17
automata processors, 24

bandwidth, 22, 30, 34, 38, 50, 64
banks, 6
big data, 17

cache, 6, 33, 37
cache coherence, 31
cache replacement, 35
Catapult project, 23
central processing unit, 13
CMOS, 5
Coffee Lake, 28
coherence protocol, 15
communication overhead, xiii
concurrency, 4
consistency model, 15
Cortex-A75, 30
CPU, 85
Cray, 41, 43
CUDA, 9, 11, 18, 84

dark silicon, 3
datacenters, 70
DDR3, 45
DDR4, 16

Dennard, Robert, 2
Dennard scaling, 2, 4
digital signal processors, 26
distributed memory, 72
DRAM, 7, 22
DVFS, 6
dynamic power, 5

eDRAM, 7, 14, 16
exascale, xiii, 11, 42, 67, 92

FinFET, 5, 15
Flynn, Michael, 13
Fortran with coarrays, 44
FPGA, 10, 23, 82, 85

GDDR5, 45
global memory, 22
Google, 27
GPU, 10, 11, 16, 27, 29, 35, 40, 45, 51, 82, 84, 85

heterogeneous system architecture, 85
high-bandwidth memory, 22
hyperthreading technology, 3, 28
HyperTransport, 40

IBM, 14
Intel, 23, 28, 42
interconnect, 35
Internet of Things, 67

last-level cache, 14

memory hierarchy, 6, 35
microarchitecture, 49
Microsoft, 23
MIMD, 17
Moore, Gordon, 2
Moore's law, 2, 4
MPI, 72
MRAM, 14
multicore, 3, 4, 10, 11, 14, 17, 28, 34, 35, 49,
    51, 67
multiple instruction–multiple data, 13
multiple instruction–single data, 13
multiprogramming environment, 6
mutlicore, 10

near-data processing, 91
networks on-chip, 34
neuromorphic chips, 25, 92
nonuniform cache access, 6, 14
nonuniform memory access, 6
Noyce, Robert, 2
NUCA, 16
NVIDIA, 11, 18, 29, 40, 85
NVIDIA Kepler, 45
NVLink, 18, 40
NVM, 7

Omni-Path, 42
OpenACC, 70, 83
OpenCL, 9, 78, 79
OpenMP, 9, 10, 70, 76, 79
optimizing compilers, 6

PCIe, 16, 18, 40, 45
PCM, 14
petascale, 11
photonics, 39
POWER9, 15
processing-in-memory, 91
programmability, 67
PThreads, 9, 11, 88

Qualcomm, 30
quantum computing, 27, 67, 95

ReRAM, 14

secure processing unit, 31
security, 46
shared memory, 76
silicon on insulator, 5
SIMD, 17
simultaneous multithreading, 2, 3,
    34
single instruction–multiple data, 13
single instruction–single data, 13
Skylake, 28
SMT, 14, 16
Snapdragon, 30
special function units, 22
speculative execution, 2
SPMD, 13, 79
SRAM, 7
streaming multiprocessor, 11, 18
streaming processors, 18, 79
STTRAM, 14
Sunway, 45
supercomputers, 43, 70
superscalar, 2
symmetrical multithreading, 14
system memory, 22
system-on-chip, 30

TaihuLight supercomputer, 45
tensor processing unit, 27
threading building blocks, 87
thread migration, 4
Titan supercomputer, 45

Unified Parallel C, 44

Verilog, 23
VHDL, 23
virtual address space, 19
virtualization, 68
virtual memory, 6
Volta architecture, 19

Xilinx, 23

Author's Biography

Mohamed Zahran

Mohamed Zahran received his Ph.D. in electrical and computer engineering from the University of Maryland at College Park in 2003. He is currently a faculty member with the Computer Science Department, Courant Institute of Mathematical Sciences at New York University (NYU). His research interest spans several aspects of computer architecture, such as architecture of heterogeneous systems, hardware/software interaction, and Exascale computing. Zahran is a senior member of IEEE, a senior member of ACM, and a member of Sigma Xi Scientific Honor Society. Besides research and teaching, he is also interested in the history and philosophy of science and *used* to be a good chess player!

You can follow him on

LinkedIn. https://www.linkedin.com/in/mzahran/

Twitter. https://twitter.com/MohamedMZahran

His webpage. http://www.mzahran.com